## Acknowledgement

"O Thou Almighty, Benevolent, Incorporeal God, Supreme Soul, My Baba, Embodiment of grace, purity and love! "Accept my multi-million thanks to make me able to do this job efficiently. As the whole knowledge narrated in the book is imparted by you on me, if any mistake unintentionally made by me please forgive and guide me so I can make correction in next edition.

With the heartfelt gratitude I wish thanks to Shri NK Mehta who translated my book in English language taking care of my emotions and vision, he has performed the job very nicely. As he was the first person to read my pre published book sincerely, I was raring to know his view about the book and he blessed me by writing a foreword for book.

I am also grateful to express my special thanks to my special daughter Garima who always reminded me indirectly that I am doing a great work by writing this book. I also extend my gratitude to all those divine souls who contributed to this work anonymously.

Dr. Sushila Choudhary

## FORWARD

Dr Sushila Choudhary was a complete stranger to me when just about a month and a half back she approached me by some reference, for getting her work entitled "अनुभूत सत्य" translated into English.

After a brief discussion I cursorily glanced at the script and took up the assignment assuring her that I would complete the task at my earliest and further that I hope that the translated version would be the closest to what she was expecting it to be up there in her mind. I added that my renderings were usually creative in character rather than being just dull and drab mechanical or literal versions.

I have since completed the task satisfactorily and now I have been asked by Dr Sushila Choudhary to write a note on the script (in the nature of a preface ) since I have agreed to the proposal ,though a little hesitatingly I would be recording my considered Impressions about the work.

In this sense this note is going to be an expression of my Impressions about it.

A work like this has to be examined on three counts-
1. The subject matter or the theme
2. The treatment thereof by the author (her style etc.)
3. The message and purpose, if any.

Initially I had no idea about the background and the theme of the book, but as I read the first few pages of the script, I was able to have a working acquaintance with the broad facts of the author's life, background and career etc. as also about 'those' experiences of hers, which constitute the major part of the proposed book /work and the lesson we learn from the experiences forming the theme/thesis of the work. The resolves/ resolutions she makes on the basis of her experiences serve to form the mission of her life and career ahead are also an important thing to learn.

Now a special word about her experiences as hinted above. In fact, her experiences are "out of our body experiences"- yet how we feel and what we find if we (by some miracle) are, that is, our soul is able to leave the body and stand apart while our physical body lies below on earth soulless. The author has undergone such experience and she feels that in such a state she became the "divine soul" herself and feels extreme peace, boundless happiness and complete freedom from all bonds and feels limitless joy and delight and contentment. This for us ordinary mortals is a kind of spiritual experience.

The author's thesis is that, in fact, we the human beings are the living power houses of divine energy but since our physical bodies suffer from the negativity of the day to day life and existence, we are not able to come out of its mundane 'shell' or shackles of attachment etc. We fail to pull up our 'living powers' or the divine energies 'residing in the body' to our advantage. The result is that we fail to rise up to a higher level of consciousness or awareness and understanding and fail to realize God (or the supreme soul/ being) expressed in our soul energy. We fail to realize that our physical being/body is not the 'real reality'- it is only an illusion- mortal & transient and perishable -where as our real reality, is our soul which is immortal, imperishable and eternal.

But how we wish there could be some mode or methodology or device to cause the above -stated realization somehow comes, we will be able to enjoy the 'outside the body -bliss' of the divinity or divineness, of the super force and experience the unmixed joy and peace, love and happiness, contentment and fulfillment.

And here in this context is a heartening news, namely, that our author Dr Sushila Choudhary has not only had the good luck of experiencing the divine 'bliss' of the state of being out of the body but has also found a device/mode with which to attain the blissful spiritual experience of super energy and that methodology is the 'Rajyoga meditation training' learnt, acquired, adopted and practiced by Dr Sushila Choudhary who can be our great guide if we wish to associate Ourselves with this spiritual activity.

I quote Dr Sushila Choudhary herself in this regard in the following paragraph which will throw further light on her thesis/theme.

'My Rajyog meditational practice' is not only a journey inward to experience our essential self -but also a journey upwards- into higher consciousness going beyond the awareness of the physical body and the physical world around.... With practice I am able to perceive and experience the dimensions of pure soul consciousness beyond sound, activity and thought. In this phase or state of awareness and experience complete freedom, peace, rest and comfort is felt by me, as if I have come home to a place I truly belong and where I can most naturally and simply be'. So this, readers, is the theme/ thesis of Dr Sushila Choudhary work and in these times where –

दरे हरम पे रहे, या बुतो के पास रहे

कहीं सुकूं न मिला, हर जगह उदास रहे।

 is the situation.

It was all the more reason for seekers like the author Dr Sushila to take pains and learn the mode of reaching a higher soul consciousness and to enjoy the bliss of divine peace and happiness. And the author claims to have acquired such skill that by adopting the mode of rajyoga meditation she can even communicate with the higher/ Supreme soul/ force at her will. This is a great thing. The good news also is that our author Dr Sushila earnestly wishes that others also take to this mode of spiritual training.

Now why has she chosen this mode or methodology is nobody's business to ask about. It is her personal matter and her personal choice. Everybody has his own God, own way of going about this quest.

Now all this much was about the theme/thesis of the book under reference. And now as for the treatment of the subject I cannot resist the temptation of saying that right from her first divine experience down to all the subsequent experience, the style or narration skill of the author has been Superb. Her narratives is homely, direct and honest, coming straight from the heart with no external trappings .The Reader is taken in and to carried away by her narration flow which arrests, as it were, the attention and emotion of the Reader.

It again goes to the credit of the writer that with her simple artless art of story-telling, she is able to weave with words, 'an out of the body 'experience of other worldliness, a strange mysterious world bordering almost on the Supernatural plane and an ceria, haunted and a weird sort of atmosphere in harmony with the theme.

We are more than once transported into strange far- away spaces, peopled with dead-bodies, mortal frames, of a Shining Star, soul energy vibrations, Journeys through vast spaces, dark frightening tunnels and interplay of darkness and light, galaxies of angelic figures and what not.     You are intrigued into a state of willing suspension of disbelief that you are 'you'.

And all this is to realize that they are just not mere bodies, but are 'living powers' residing in these bodies and this realization may come through her Rajyog meditation training.

Going through the last part of work we gather that there is still 'further higher dimensions' to her mission and that is self transformation and self transformation of not some small lot, but of all the human beings of this planet by making them aware of their true real selves. They need to be reminded that love, peace, contentment, values etc are qualities basically ingrained in their personalities. The only need is to rediscover them themselves. There is no better way than this to make this world a better place to live in to make the entire world humanity more enlightened through her Rajyog meditation spiritual training. In this sense this work of hers is a spiritual Saga with a sublime purpose.

I had told you in the beginning, readers , that Dr. Sushila was a complete stranger to me when she had first visited me sometime back. I do not know whether after going through and working on her the script under review, through past sometimes, I can still hold on to the same position !

Anyhow, I must at this stage advert to my initial reaction to the contents of the script what I was inclined to conclude that this work of Dr. Sushila ji was essentially a personal document only seeking to relate the ways to her own growth and development & seeking clues to her own peace, happiness and contentment only.

But No! when my readings of the script reached the stage of the last few pages, I had to revise my opinion, as I suddenly realised that the work had a 'social face' also, for the writer Dr Sushila Choudhary does not propose to limit her mission to her own growth, development and happiness alone but is also thinking on a higher plane, a larger purpose, a nobler mission, in as much as she wants Rajyog meditation mode to be employed for the upliftment of the young generation also.
Her mission is more pious. She wants to equip them with what is known as value based self empowerment, and in this sense than the work has an educational facet also, and as such the work under review is an enlightening educational document also, Dr. Sushila ji wants their students and young minds.

Be that as it may my good wishes and compliments to her on her unflinching commitment to a great cause.

N. K. Mehta R. E. S
37,Income Tax Colony
Paota C Road Jodhpur
Phone 9928040740, 02912540740

Dated 30th April 2017

PREFACE
I feel myself auspicious that I have been requested to say something about Doctor Sushila Choudhary a divine personality with attractive aura influences the person within minutes comes in her vicinity positively.

I met her first time when she got posted in ESI Hospital as a pediatrician in 2002 August. In first look even I found her as a simple, sober, egoless and a Cooperative person. As I was a gynecologist and needs a pediatrician during deliveries her posting given me a lot of relief and boosted my work as gynecologist to carry out more deliveries at ESI Hospital with availability of such a sincere pediatrician.

She looking after her job very sincerely whether it's caring of newborn, immunization or admission of children in her ward and taking all care by herself from nursing to resident doctor and as a specialist because at that time there was no nursing staff trained in taking care of newborn infants and children below 10 years age in that hospital so every work she was doing her own very sincerely and enthusiastically.

She used to come in my chamber after 12 noon as there were few patients only in OPD as referral stopped after 12 noon by dispensaries to learn about ESI scheme and its working as I was posted there since 2004 as Superintendent. During these meetings I found that she is totally a different personality, her attitude about any situation and problem is always solving type and most of time she give significance to self responsibility to do and fulfill any plan or action while taking in hand.

One day she told me that you are not a female you are energy, living energy source residing in this body and you are operating this body system by using your thought power in response to stimuli coming from physical senses like eyes, ear, touch, taste, smell etc. She explained me this all with such a practical attitude that the same moment I realised this is truth of life. I felt her aura is always powerful that within few days I meant that above principle had activated and begun to reflect in my thinking and my attitude. By this I felt myself much stronger and lighter at the workplace then before. I realised that 'yes, all human beings are similar beings and child of one God' I also felt that kindness compassion and respect for others are gradually increasing than before in my attitude because of her company. This all knowledge she imparted about soul and

Supreme soul (Power) made me feel very practical and truthful in day to day life.

There after I begun to help her in her projects related to Rajyog and spirituality in health fields and I was witness of all the events explained by her in this book held at ESI Hospital the family planning study, the thalassaemia study, the miracles happening with patients. It's all her company that motivated me to hold the promise that I will also live life since the day in future on principle of soul consciousness and became a regular Rajyog practitioner.

During my Rajyog practice one day I heard a voice telling me that why are you worrying I am here with you. when I looked all around I saw a very beautiful, pleasant, divine sparkling star few feets away from me and giving me a very lovable soothy feeling and all that sound waves I observed coming from this star, I was just amazed, blessed by seeing this scene and lost within it and found myself at that moment very pleased, blessed, light, contented at every level. The scene lasted for a minute but in my memory it printed forever. Now I got an internal conscience that yes the knowledge and experience all explained by doctor Sushila is a truth and if this be realised by all human beings it will convert community and world in a happy, blessed, divine civilization.

I wish this message of her in form of this book will reach each and every soul of world so everyone can encounter her or him real self and can bring change in his destiny by knowing the secrets of life, karm philosophy and power of thoughts of human mind. God bless her all success

Dr Suman Chauhan Gynecologist Jodhpur

My encounter with truth

May God bless his soul with peace, or his soul is wandering.. Strayed away from its path...., It is his/her ghost that is harassing all..., Somebody's soul resides in that bungalow, it does not let others live there etc. etc.
 These are some sentences the like of which we often hear and have been hearing right from our childhood. Are they true, or they are just hoax as just imagination or myth.
It is natural for such questions to arise in our minds and then after a little thinking over or pondering over the matter, one would give his/her verdict or decision. "No, it is all bogus." "There is nothing like 'aatma-vatma', it is customary to speak like that and so I have mentioned it

in this way." "It is all bunkum." Another person would say something like this, "We have felt/experienced anything like this ever"...still third person would say 'Yes it is true, it is a fact, I have experienced it myself...' Or yet another person would report he/she used to be harassed by her own relative soul... But not now... Certain rituals were carried out and her soul has stopped tormenting or harassing now... Thanks to those rituals or procedures.

So these would be the normal reactions on these issues: the soul.

 But then, now, let me take you through a 'felt truth' in order to find an answer to all these questions and thereafter yours doubts etc. on the subject would be cleared and not only this, but further you will be able to have a 'live interview, a one-to-one talk with your own self and please take it that this is my firm belief.

But before we embark on this journey of experiences, I would like to have some small conversation with you, for if, we want to know about and understand the subject, our mind and our own sense of discretion, our reasoning, our wisdom and our intellect or intelligence, our sense of judgment should be fully ready and prepared. Clarity of mind, impartiality, boldness and objectivity - all these are the first pre-conditions of accepting the truth irrespective of whether the subject is that of Science or Medical Science or of Spirituality

.Being a medicine-person myself, I can realize how important is this.

 Now may I put it to you "Have you yourself ever seen this earth moving on its axis or making rounds speedily in the orbit.

'No' would be your answer, isn't it? Although we know earth is round and it moves on its own axis and the orbit also. And we can practically explain this thing to others also, for those people who went into the space and from there they witness the earth, they could actually observe that the earth is round and it moves around with a speed. Now it is this observation and experience of those scientists that we took to be a first hand proof and could confirm the truth about earth's shape and movement and accordingly could practically use them there after in our further experiments.

The five senses of ours which are a part and parcel of our body are not sharp enough to clearly apprehend and comprehend all mysteries and activities of nature. To take an example from our day to day life- we have felt several times that there are some persons in whose company we feel great peace and comfort and Solace but as against it there are certain others whose presence or company or talks, we would like to avoid for the fear that we may not have to face anger or humiliating situations and an undignified, unwanted, unwelcome and uncomfortable atmosphere. Now who helps us in anticipating a friendly atmosphere or in anticipating an uncomfortable- certainly not our five karmic senses, but our sense of perception, our mind and our intellect which serves as a true guide in apprehending and comprehending the total situation at a given moment of time. I think you all would agree that our heart and our mind is sometime happy and other times a little some sad. It warns us, at times of some coming event or danger, some unknown fears, also disturbs us at times, and upset.

Would you let me know, in which or what part of our body is our, what we call, the "Mann" is situated ?

As a doctor I have studied the entire constitution and composition of the human body. But nowhere has the situation/ Landmark of "मन" been taught to us in our medical lectures of course, although parallel or similar words like Heart (Dil), Liver(Jigar) are often used as meaning of Mann in common language. But they are all misleading, neither the heart nor liver have the capability to 'think or understand'. And even in the brain which is the physical matter inside body, here also everything is done by means of impulses, driven by chemical receptors.

Where the 'thought energy' originates from? Where is it conserved or collected and how does it work or operate ? There is no account of or answers to all these questions in the science of the body (physiology) or the medical science itself.

Through the pages of this book I seek to relate my experience of being /travelling /moving outside my body and I wish to take you along with me on this journey so that you may know in a better way how, when and in what way I reached this invisible world, or call it the "Sukshmalok" or metaphysical energy world- and what I really felt.

From, here is, our journey to invisible world starts. But, before you accompany me, you have to make yourself detached from your physical body at your thought level because only then, you can see impartially that how our mind, the thoughts drive our five senses or this body as a vehicle.

Here let me talk for awhile and let me introduce myself in order to let you appreciate the whole project in a better perspective.

I was raised and brought up in a middle class family. The evils prevalent in family and social life or society like giving woman a lower status than man, a subordinate position, to take it as a man's birthright to torture woman, to just 'use' woman as a 'thing' and addiction, abuse language too as of matter of male right - and all that goes by the name of male chivalry or chauvinism. To experience all this plus the family problems, the aspect of adjusting with the different temperaments of different people in the family and the ego-clashes raising their heads up on various occasion over just small trifling things - I had been a witness to all these ego-clashes all through my childhood.

I had left hopes of my life being happy-story. Feeling of grudge and jealousy nursed against the entire male community had crept in long back. Life had turned to be a hopeless dream. But still, on some strong moments I picked up courage from some corner in my heart to hope against hope and to resolve to stand on my on legs, by remaining /staying indifferent to all that I was surrounded by - and if possible to free the society from evils, it suffered from. I strongly felt and resolved that I should do no such act by deed, by word of mouth or my conduct that may ruin my chances of the peace of mind, for if, I fail to do so I shall not be even in a position to gain my self-independence.

During my medical studies I met Dr. Harendra and from the way he talked and behaved and conducted himself I had to change my opinion about 'men' and began to think that all the males are not alike and that there are some males at least who consider women on equal footing and who are thoughtful enough to believe in giving due regards to women. But within a year of the marriage this belief began to shake off and my belief in the male-goodness fell like a house of cards, and on the other hand it became stronger and stronger as I began to think the males not only don't regard as women worthless, and object of no value, but using all the uncanny ways - saam, daam, dand, bhed - make it a point to just crush the simplicity, the delicacy of their being. I came to believe firmly that they are past masters in this cruel art and can do anything, can manoeuvre anything to destroy the woman's identity, notwithstanding whatever name their relationship is known by or given.

My disgust for how shabbily I has been treated and how cruel was the race called men, turned into a feeling of complete detachment or alienation from life. In the middle of all this I gave birth to a girl child after just one and half year of my marriage. In the course of delivery of this child, she developed a mental sub normality due to wants of adequate amount of oxygen. It was thought as if that the entire cause of this was I and that the entire responsibility of bringing up the child was mine alone. My life become filled with question marks, misery, problems and life with no peace. Peace became a foreign world so far as I was concerned.

In such a situation I would wonder whether God or some external super power would hear my woes and redress my grievances. All kind of questions would rise up in my mind and I would expect some answer of them by some competent power. Who has made this world? If human being were created, why is there so much variation in their nature, in their temperaments? What is the right manner of living a life? Why should I alone tolerate, suffer out of all? When I don't want to take revenge for what is happening to me, what is the other agency to do justice in such a case as that of mine? And why then is the agency not doing the justice in my case? Why is this world so full of evil and injustice, immorality and atrocity? Does real happiness and peace really exist in life? Is it a reality? And whether with the kind of thought in mind with which I'm proceeding - is it wrong or right? Or shall I give up caring for other and others opinion and give them a hard fitting reply - it is in the mire of these doubts that each day of my life was passing of.

May I say have that up to the age of 27 years of my life, I was a person and a personality with sound scientific attitude and belief that is to say I did believe that God was some power. Although I had no belief or faith in things like ghosts, spirits fasting or rituals like Katha, kirtan as something capable of refining our life or in supernatural powers, hoax etc. etc. They were not at all a part of my belief system. To think rationally on things connected with life and to make them a part of day-to-day life something for which I was really made.

Being a Doctor allopathic was a part of my mental makeup - but other sciences like naturopathy, acupressure, yoga and other alternative systems are also not averse to me. I would like to know or be interested in knowing the advantages of their practical use in day-to-day life was also a part of my daily routine even then. I have already told you I was an allopathic doctor no doubt, but I was never averse to other disciplines too.

I distinctly remember readers, that particular day of the year 1993. I was then posted at Kalendri in Sirohi District. I was a mother of a girl two and half year old and my husband too was posted there itself on a government job .The day was a holiday and I was at home. It was around 10.30 or 11 o'clock in the morning. I was standing up on a stool and clearing the webs made by the spider in the corners of the roof. Now as I was cleaning the spider's webs, I suddenly felt shooting pain in the left abdominal part just below the chest. The pain soon became intense and intolerable and I felt I would soon fall down as a result of the pain. For fear of getting badly hurt if I fell down, I called my husband for help, while controlling myself a little. The next moment I fell down on the double bed nearby losing my body a little. But... what is this! ? I had felt sound of my falling down on the bed but then I felt myself actually I standing about 5-6 feet above the bed and wonder of wonders - I was free of any pain whatsoever and was feeling very relaxed and light and easy. But it beat my wits to find that whole I'm lying almost like a dead person or a person not in his sense then how come I'm finding myself standing above the ground at the height of about 5-6 feet. What is this? What is all this, am I divided person - Have 'I' become a person divided into two? - One myself on the bed in my front and another I (one), up there a little above the bed where I was 'I' feeling quite alive and feeling my (separate) existence. I tried to see myself too, so much so that I went to the mirror of the dressing table of the room wanting to see myself in the mirror as to how I was looking like. But I was stunned to find /know that I'm realising myself to be happening to be there and to realise fully that I'm there, I'm thinking and am realising that I'm 'understanding' it all - but here in the mirror - I'm not able to be 'appearing' in the mirror in my own original figure or form. I am in a position to see things but I'm not able to see 'myself'. I can see the usual objects of the room - the furniture, the bed and even my body! My own body! I could also see that my husband hearing my sound for help comes there a little confused and perplexed standing near the bed trying hard to revive my body. I can see all this clearly.

And seeing all this I'm greatly upset as I seem to be asking - Is there anyone here who can help me out - Somebody tell me how come I'm finding myself in this strange condition /situation. I state this to myself with all my conviction honestly - but LOL what's this, I am not able to 'voice' all this physically, I'm not able to 'utter' what I am feeling - words, as if, are not able to come out of the throat. But believe me here when I say that I'm experiencing a feeling of great, deep 'peace' - a strange but satisfying calmness - tranquillity, a central peace in my heart of heart.

And at the same time I'm able to apprehend and know what is and has been happening with me out here - I'm aware - I'm aware that my husband is telling my body 'raise your hand - I want to take (Measure) your blood pressure' - as If I have been able to apprehend these words also from his lip-reading manner and pace - I am able to read what he is wishing to speak. I'm able to apprehend and follow all this, but what beats my wits is the thought - while I'm out and up here - then how will /could this - my body down here - raise my hand! My poor hubby cannot understand this small thing! Or that he is not able to see me? Why is he talking to that 'body' or 'frame' of mine - while the reality is this that I'm up here?

And while I was in this perplexing situation, I suddenly felt that some invisible waves having a sort of magnetic attraction have come to touch upon my head and with these I'm hearing the words - 'Do You want to know this - Do You want to know the answer?'

I mechanically and immediately said 'yes', and then from that very point was a voice - a word - come to be heard by me - 'see', as If he was giving me a hint to see towards my own body. I saw my own body and I felt that its outer covering had become invisible and I'm looking at the internal organs of the body in such as a way as the human anatomy is being shown /exhibited

/seen through a glass-case. I felt at the same time that those magnetic waves had now vanished. I began to watch my body and it's each and every system was being seen by me - my lungs, kidneys, liver, intestines and even the heart - but so- what was it! My heart was fluttering like the wings of the dying bird. The vibration of a fast movement. I could readily understand that the problem related to heartbeat had come to develop which in medical terminology is called Supraventricular tachycardia where in the heart of course begins to beat at the rate of 200-250 but is not able to pump up the blood. Thus for want of blood circulation I had developed the trouble of Ischemia, the lack or want of oxygen in that particular organ and an account of not being able to bear the pain I 'jumped out' of this body. And I let my body fall safe on the bed and what miracle - with that thought (of jumped out of the body) I felt myself at once relieved. I was feeling so good now a certain lightness - as if I'm in a state of weightlessness - so light that if I want to fly, I can fly in a minute - a sense of extreme peace - and a unique kind of delight and a contentment I felt.

I surveyed the atmosphere of the room. My husband with the aid of an associate was subjecting me (my body) to cardiac massage. His face had turned pale and he was appearing to be greatly worried. He was examining my pulse again and again and also my heartbeat - but see, I paid no heed to him, nor was I feeling just interested in any of the activities he was doing. I was perplexed as my own lightness and delight and to know this that I was shut up /imprisoned in this body and now I'm breathing freely in the open and am taking in the breath of reassurance. I was feeling extremely good. So I thought let me walk off from here to some other place and with the thought, have again the same magnetic waves, I felt, got connected with me and a sentence of command in tone was heard by me - 'stop here itself'. I wondered, a little puzzled though, 'who's this, who has come to know what had risen up in my mind and is therefore stopping me from leaving?' but is at the same time, is giving the impression that as if I'm already acquainted with this vibration and he is not somebody new for me, Obviously he is some well-wisher of mine and is reliable, worthy of trust and reliance and is eager for my good. Hence to obey he would be a must for me and my interest lies in this and while linking all this I stopped there itself. Now my attention is turned back to my state of peace and lightness and the attendant feeling of enjoyment.

And now begin to see my body and the event happening around and here I find that the face of my husband turns, at once, red with enthusiasm. In order to know the reason I look at my body, , and now I find that my heart too that was fluttering is now beating with its usual speed. The blood flow too began to be fairly adequate and so being contented, I say to myself 'oh, so now it has started functioning properly - it is good - the worry of all of them (my husband and other associates) is over.' But so soon this expression of satisfaction is over, the same invisible magnetic waves found upon me and asks 'So are you now satisfied!' I understand it right that is referring to the recovery of the functioning of my body. And again the same thing I say with satisfaction 'yes'. There upon the commanding voice is again heard to say 'Then come' and on hearing this command - my existence of at a height of 5 to 6 feet disappears /vanishes from the scene.

I suddenly find myself very heavy or weighty and tired at the same time that I am once again shut up in the body lying on the bed. I am feeling too weak in the upper part of my body. I then slowly open my eyes and become miserable to think that I am once again shut up in the body - which is giving me a feeling of being trapped in a cage. The peace, the naturalness, the carefree feeling, the lightness of that outer existence are tempting me on the one hand and my eyes are filled with tears of the thought that I'm not able to quit. I am perplexed at the thought of my strange situation - This what has happened with me. Are my tears real or are they a part of my invisible situation? I try to touch my eyes but my hand soon falls down as I raise it, I feel great weakness, my husband seeing my unhealthful state tries to console me ' Don't worry - you are well. All will be well by and by. You better take rest.'

In this way, this 1 to 2 minute episode changed my very attitude towards life. All my earlier beliefs fell like house of cards; now I was lying in my bed quietly and was thinking, have I reborn after attaining death? Is this called "Death" and if it so, then it is a very transient (momentary) and delightful event. Thinking all this over, my fear of death as if had come to an end, rather to me it appeared even a little romantic. For three to four days thereafter, I took medicines including glucose bottles etc. after getting well I wanted to tell my husband about recent experience and episode but he paid no attention to them and on the other end started telling me that "sometimes lack of oxygen can create visual hallucinations – you better forget all this and do not repeat it." Whereas the fact is that I had lived each and every moment of the episode with full consciousness, awareness. I had experienced every part of the event almost live. I knew it that it was no illusion and I have being aware of everything that was around me – every object, every sound, every voice, each feeling – plus I had been understanding, the whole thing, including the fact that people would not believe me and as such I had stopped talking about it to the people. But I had started looking for an explanation of the phenomenon that had taken place in my case, i.e. what had happened with me for this purpose, I consulted books on religion, science, Hindu scriptures etc. with the thought in my mind that there might be some other persons who may have undergone an experience like the mine – but except in the Geeta I did not find any proper explanation/rational/clue. I made broad references in this behalf to Quran, Bible and a few other religious books – but no I failed to get a satisfactory clue on parallel.

My curiosity did not stop here and I started every day trying to take myself back into the same situation mentally in which I had been thrown in earlier. I tried to imagine that I am in the invisible form and I am out of my body. In the beginning I started laughing at myself – rather amused as to what I was doing or trying to do – isn't it madness, I thought – but after about 2-3 attempts I found that I am in my body itself – but yet by thinking so I started feeling light, more reassured and good. I became free of all the worldly things – and it is strange that I started having a unique feeling of that peace and joy. Now I started repeating this practice tempting to address that invisible power and ask it as to "Who you are? Where are you? and since it is you alone who knows about this mystery, I want to meet you and see you. Kindly listen to my prayer and get in touch with me once again. "

Its practice and attempt on my part went on for quite some time where after one night I was not able to sleep, sitting by the window and looking out towards sky and gazing stars, was at the same time recollecting that experience of mine and to think of and remember that invisible power and addressing it and saying "when you are very much somewhere then why does my voice not reach you now? Why don't you answer me? I have to put so many questions, so many queries I have to make. Please do contact me as soon as you can." It should have been about 3-4am of the night, suddenly as if in a flash I felt that a star of light flashed over my forehead and it moved on through my entire body frame – right up to the toe of my foot and suddenly it sort of flew out and I felt that I began to fly out too along with it while "my body" was still sitting on the bed only, I with my (minute existence) sukshma self, like on the earlier occasion felt that I was out there but now in form of that star. The same feeling of peace, lightness, joy and contentment had over taken me once again, I felt elated that I was flying "riding" that star with the speed of a rocket – but not knowing with what aim, what goal, in what direction – and to what destination etc. I was feeling as if somebody was drawing me towards it, I literally "saw" my journey. And in a moment I found myself out of my room and out there reaching in the world of sky, moon, stars and I was even going further advancing – but then suddenly I sought of stopped, for I found myself passing through a dark tunnel – the sky, the stars all had been left behind. My speed was very fast. I was feeling a bit frightened to pass through a dark tunnel like that – but then suddenly I found that I had crossed the tunnel and was out of it –

but Oh My ! What is this...? I had got into a place with red light where this red light was spread all over and all around. It was a place very calm and peaceful and with very supportive ambience. I suddenly reached now a place which was something like that of a cinema hall – where there was a certain definite place for everybody to sit and with very low or dim light. I felt as if many others like me were also sitting there and they were all there on their appointed places but – they were noticed by me only in the form of "stars". There were no physical stools etc. there but in the form of stars they were all in their prescribed places, line wise. I wondered where my place was. When suddenly a beam of light as if began to show me my place – It was in the third line from the front. Flabbergasted and perplexed I went on and got stuck – settled. I began to realize that everything there was systematic and orderly. Now I tried to know who all these are and why are they here, why have they come? I began to see, as if, in the front and my back. I soon felt and realized that the sitting arrangement there was as per their "shine." The more shining ones were occupying the front lines and those with less "shine" were sitting respectively on the rear. There were numberless stars, there out of which, to some I was able to recognize as my friends, relatives or acquaintances. The next I found that everybody's attention was focused towards the front and everybody is lost being busy in seeing – just as what happens in our cinema halls, films - I looked in front to where I found that a unique star was shining – no, it was not just a star – it was some waterfall of pleasant coolness, of love, of joy and delight of supreme bliss. The light of star is very bright but not encroaching the vision, the showers of the fall are drenching our very being with a feeling of love and joy – what a lovely and blissful sight it was. I got lost to in watching that incredible scene. I felt as if I am into a moment of all that is called true love all that is called true faith, peace and delight and joy and I wanted to "live" that moment and live it wholly, fully, richly, and perpetually. I wished that time stopped here for even this moment to turn into eternity. I had never tasted the tang of this kind of happiness ever before. I was also realizing that we spent our whole life in pursuit of all these things for happiness, for such true love and peace and aspirations but neither we are able to apprehend that nor we know the ways – the correct ways of achieving them. I felt I do not need anything in my life any more. I felt as if the last and the ultimate thing has been achieved and that I am fully contented – my thirst for happiness has come to be quenched. The more I see towards that star, the more joyful, happy and contended am I feeling! Yes, I thought and wished that only if I had been there in the first line, in front of the screen! in that case I could have been even further nearer to that star and the rays or beam of light emitting from the star would have been brighter more adequate and sharper and more powerful. With this wish in my mind I felt a mild streak of grief and then suddenly I felt that a few waves of light from that divine star came down up to me and as they touched me I felt that certain words emitting from it were asking me " Do you wish to come in the front line?" when I said "yes" then the word that I heard were; 'for that you will have to study further, you will have to work hard.' To which I answered rather puzzled – "I like studies, I have studied fairly enough already but if you tell me so, I would pursue them further – I shall try hard – I shall leave no stone unturned as I have to be (sit) in the front line." And in response to this came a valley of words – "then it is alright – go and study further." And with these words, what do I find?! – I find the whole thing having vanished. Puzzled, perplexed I was, I found myself sitting back on my bed. Puzzled I was just to think or remember or recollect that it was the set of those very magnetic sounds, vibrations that I have earlier felt when I have stepped out of my body. This was the sharpness of that very voice/ power! The same orders, the same consultative tones, the same warmth of emotions, the same homeliness – isn't that I have come back on having met the same "power" whom I had longed wished to see and meet once? Oh yes, right I am. It is the same "power" but I never thought that it would be in the form of a "star" – a star full of life-force, of energy – a perennial source of love,

peace and supreme bliss, oh' what "joy" was there –
supreme joy it was, strange, unique, unparalleled and
yet beautifully peaceful and peacefully beautiful. But
does it stay so far away from here – and it takes only a
fraction of seconds for us to reach over there and then
how forceful, powerful it is! How irresistible is that
power – its words have the power, ability, capacity to
create scene and circumstances and cause removal /
disappearance of things. This power cannot do any
harm to others – it is something positive, it exists where
it is to help and cause happiness to others.
Now I was on my bed with yet another superhuman,
transient experience. I got concerned as I thought that I
have to gain the benefit or privilege of getting
proximate, getting nearer to this power – that divine
star. But the point is what are those additional studies
that this power wants me to undertake and to be adapt
so as to enable me to be worthy of its favour. I was, in
fact, regretting why I had not myself asked it as to what
studies to undertake or what college to go to or what
books to read. The fact perhaps is that on meeting, on
listening, on experiencing that power I am so
overwhelmed with contentment of joy that forget all
other things.
I had, of course, by now understood that kind of studies
desirable at this stage are not the ones that are to be
had at some worldly college or from some books and
these studies can be prosecuted or pursued only at

places or with people or books connected with that supreme power called Parmatma or God.

Now by and by I began to try to get in touch with various religions, monasteries, seats and their followers or their teachers or masters in order to know or learn of and from their experiences that may just give me a suggestion as regards that power and if so I might began to take up the studies, I am talking about, there, that is ,as those place or with those persons but no – I went everywhere – Gurudwara, temples, mosque, Jain upashrayas, churches and graveyards – I got no clue to my search anywhere to my utter dismay.

Tired of all this, then, I began to take again to my meditation method reflecting over at home itself. To recreate in the mind that earlier experience, that scene I used to experience great peace and power. I would meditate and would tell that invisible star - 'now you please show me the way by leading on which I can reach you and meet you.'

 About two years passed in this manner when I happened to come to Jodhpur. Here my younger sister had already got connected with a certain institution and driven by the education and the attraction of the institution, she had decided to renounce the worldly life and not to get married, as well. Then I asked by my mother to talk to the sister on the above issue and I sat down to discuss the matter with her. At this she asked me to hear what she had to say about that institution as to what she had learnt there and attained only then I should ask her to disclose her mind and to take her decision in the matter.

She began telling and I, on my part kept hearing her silently. I was stunned to find that every word of what she was telling was appearing true to me. I felt, it appeared as if she was analysing and explaining all those metaphysical experiences of mine which I had undergone. For two days, twelve hours this discussion went on. By now I was convinced that some invisible power had been directing in what was going on and then towards the end of the discussion she, my sister - told me, 'Now, you tell me whether my decision is right or not?' To which I said- 'Absolutely right' and also told to my mother that - 'let her do whatever she thinks the right course is, I would approve it and shall give her my full support'. There upon my sister told me, 'You too join this institution, here God himself does the teaching'. But I couldn't accept this very statement of hers. I told her, 'Look, I now know God too well but today's world is replete with such places where God is practised as a profession, and what sense are not committed in the name of God & God's pure commercialisation. They claim that they themselves are God and the God gives his blessings to all through them. In fact to be frank I don't have any faith in such people or such institution.'

Having said all this I came back to my work place Sirohi. But days were passing over with the big question in mind - God knows when shall I know the detail of the studies & then when I shall I be able to get into the proximity of that divine power which I have been wishing for ardently all these months. One day while meditating over that power I felt that having been turned into a star, I was traveling out of this body and have reached the Hills of Mt. Abu. There was one Doctor's conference over there, all others were busy with the conference, while I have reached the institution referred to by my sister in there, I was meeting persons clad in white and I was feeling so good.

After a few months of this vision that I saw, I actually got (1997) an invitation from a doctor classmate of mine who worked in the same institution urging upon me, to attend a conference (at Abu) and I thought to myself that this episode of invitation to me was surely pre-ordinance by that power in the very thought idea of going there went that I was going to 'live' much awaited moment.

I along with my husband and my children started for going to the conference. My younger sister's words echoed in my mind again and again - Yes, those words - 'You come here too, here God himself teaches us.' I was feeling that these words had the elements of truth in it - but still the mind, the intellect was not at all ready to accept the truth behind these words. At last in this state of doubt, I remembered and recalled in my mind and heart the invisible star, telling that - "I consider you alone as the Supreme power and God above all, as there cannot be several Gods and I wonder if it is you who are really working as the actual spirit behind this institution. And if that is right, it is you, yourself, who will have to tell me the truth about it - for, I will not believe on things and facts told by others and all this I'm telling you in confidence, exclusively and exclusively to you, that the sole purpose of my going to this conference is to search you, find you, discover you, to apprehend you, to get to you and nothing else - nothing whatsoever."

The conference was a two day affair and passing through the various sessions, talks, discussions, eating and drinking and moving around visiting places worth seeing, the time just passed by how we just don't know. Apart from medical subject, The people connected with the institution told us that - spiritualism is also considered as a concern for leading a stress free, disease free life and the life full of happiness.

I visited the various places connected with the institution and tried to know who founded the institution and how. Having known this my thoughts turned another thoughts - namely (that) whether the power that runs the entire world and universe has founded this institution and that too with a special purpose or goal, my intellectual mind was not prepared to accept this but on the other hand voice from the innermost core of my heart came to the effect that the pure vibes of this place favours the concept & if it is so then it must be the same power whom I have already met and again if it is so then that power itself will have to give proof to me that (Yes) it is the same power that is directing me and is the one which is directing the institute also.

However, the most important point and the big question was: how or in what manner it would do it or express it or reveal it? For after all it is out there in the space in the form of a wide-awake, observant, resplendent star, so what next now - what will happen? Time was passing fast, the time for returning from there was approaching quick and my mind was beginning to be filled in a strange discomfort - I was experiencing the presence of an unconscious mind in there, which had it appeared, risen up or awaken and was telling me - if I don't find (or see) the Supreme power even here, then where (else) would I find it? Whether I have done the right efforts in having, tried to see /find 'it here'. Let me add here that I had become adamant on the point that if somebody told me that this institution had been set up by God, I wouldn't accept the statement.

The question then next arises is, how is that power - super power - then going after all to contact me - establish connection with me? It must be requiring some medium at least to get in touch with me. Is there or can there be any prescribed medium, appointed time or place which I may come to know if in advance and then I put it (the power) to test?

Pondering over and reflecting upon all this I do not know how the night had marched in. All I know is that I wasn't getting sleep and the time was around 3 or 4 AM, my mind has been so upset and as if a breaking point had come. I was getting impatient - felt like I should cry, cry rather loud. The thought of that divine power was tormenting me, feeling tortured I was telling it in my mind 'when are you going to solve my problems? Please unravel this puzzle, this riddle soon.'

And this thought of mine was interrupted suddenly when I was reminded of the fact that told by my younger sister that -everyday in the morning in this institution 'great thoughts' mahavakyas of that divine super power are recited and the person who recites these mahavakya great thoughts at that time serves as a medium to that divine power - the supreme grace. In other words, the supreme power itself which directs or governs this institution causes the mahavakya class to be held. As this thought clicked my mind at once I became calm and relaxed and finishing my daily chores hurriedly, I rushed on to this place where this mahavakya class was to be held and I reached there before the time.

God knows what drew me so excitedly to the place and what fascination was there in that place and to that my heart began to beat fast,  as happens with a young girl while on her 'first date' with her boyfriend- her object of love - had I become a girl of this kind age, I thought to myself! Whatever it may have been but, for one thing, I felt as if I am totally surrendering myself to the machinations of this situation. A big upsetting of mind, a lot of excitement and the attendant impatience- that was what my mind frame was getting to become. This was being accompanied by an ardent wish, a passionate desire and a sharp chill of anticipation/ expectation and a vow to the effect that if I do not find / meet that supreme power today, I would never seek it here. While I was still lost in these thoughts, I found that an old sister of the place had reached there and she occupies the place/seat which is earmarked for the person who is to recite the mahavakya of that day. She has a printed paper in her hand which is read over to the audience every day. My problem to worry increases at the thought that if the old women started to read out the paper directly - what would happen and who would answer my queries? They would remain unanswered.

I now began to talk in my mind to that supreme power as usual "look this is the last chance, and last moment when you can convince me that it is you who are doing this work (of running this institution) – otherwise I will quit this place without telling anybody that. But this much is certain that you are the supreme most power in this world and there is none else more powerful than you. But- you've to prove it 'sir'– yes, you've to."

With this working of my mind - with this mental conversation, with this thought process in the mind, I threw a quick glance at the class. All the regular students present there were dressed in pure white clothes. I was the only exception sitting in a different dress and on a separate sofa on one side of the hall. All the regular students were sitting on a white cloth sheet spread on the floor.

And then the class started and the old women without lifting the paper put the first question to the class – "whom is the supreme god remembering today?" There upon I felt like shouting and say - "me, to me and to me alone and none else - for it is I who had been calling you all through the night."  But I could not speak all this outwardly - because my aim/goal was different.

In reply to her question different answers came forth for instance, "To some yogi soul" or "To an innocent & pure child" from the class. The old women then spoke, "No, God today is remembering that child who is remembering him (god) with all its heart and soul but now after reaching here it wants to come out in outer world of pain, lie and vices. But the God almighty is telling that soul; this outer world - this worldly world is no good, it is all false, full of perversions. You should stay here under my tutelage, umbrella and eye safe and secure. If you turn your face towards that false world, you'll find yourself in great grief, trouble and you'll regret. So stay here ever in the divine lap of love of godfather, don't leave it ever".

As these words fell in my ears, I realised it is the same voice, same vibration which I've earlier perceived in my two earlier episodes of experiences - a typical experience- the same sound - vibrations emanating from that star - and hearing that very intensely or shall I say that it is the same voice - the voice of that very phenomenon.

Even as listening to those words my mind became suddenly so calm, reassured rather my entire impatience, concern, anger- in a moment as if melted away and vanished - god knows where. I felt as if a few seconds back I had been burning in the nasty fire of emotions and undergoing the torture of self-immolation as it were, but the sound waves of the star that appeared on the scene had embalmed my tormented mind to peace and had vanished away. And now indeed my mind was feeling a sense of extreme delight and limitless joy - joy beyond any measure, delight beyond all degrees. My mind now had a strong desire - irresistible desire to go and embrace the old women hard, and for the old women, at the moment, to me seemed to be the reflection of (that) divine star. And with those words of the old women I felt in my heart and mind an extreme peace, calm, tranquillity and contentment. The same feeling that I had undergone or realised/experienced 'that particular day' when I had encountered the divine star in that superhuman (transcendental) world to which I was led by the divine light, tears flooded out of my eyes - tears of regret? - But why regret – Yes, here my intellect - my sense of wisdom and discretion- began to put my conscience to shame - but what and why shame? Shame at my mean attempt to put that supreme power to test. How great and loving 'He' is that he has respected my wish - had I gone away from here without knowing /meeting visiting Him I would have been a terrible loser. I would have lost him and lost my own good fortune forever. Yes, these tears of regret had now left me with an unprecedented joy, delight and a heart sublimated by pure regret and now I came out of the class since the old women had now begun to read out that paper and my aim or objective had been since realised.  I was almost mad with joy. I was on top of the world and I was feeling as if I had discovered or obtained the most priceless and precious treasures of the world - like the treasure of Karoon.

In the next scene I find myself proceeding in my car with my family towards Kalendri with closed eyes, while sitting at the back seat, I was trying to recapture on my mind the scene that I had left behind - the scene of the class - I was recapturing as to how I had got at last, the solution to my problem, plus the thought with a sense of wonder as to how full of energy this entire chain of events had been. I was of course living in my usual way of life, yet I had been feeling a sense of what may be called an 'other worldliness' in me - my own self or say a sense of being in a territory of boundless energy with fully supply of life-force.

After this phase was over I felt by and by, like returning in my thoughts to my present existence.

 And again I felt a streak of doubt encroaching upon my mind or intellect (as was my usual temperament) namely, as to how could I be satisfied in that class that the divine power ,the supreme divine power in the form of the old lady had assured to me in particular? Particularly because if she had addressed to me she should normally have asked my name, demanded my introduction etc. Which she did not do then how did I take it that her words were meant for me in particular, specially used for me etc. These negative thoughts as if in a moment, took away from me all my joy and happiness. I had been experience hitherto before.

I got agitated again and addressed that divine power in these words: you are a guileless, simple being, kind and remover of other people's sorrow, then why do I every time, I have a feeling that you are not revealing or unfolding 'the whole truth' to me. Why do you refrain yourself from doing so? Why are my heart, my mind, my wisdom and intellect filled with a certain 'incompleteness'?

With these, remembering That Power with all my heart I began to cry. Here then I felt that those sound waves are getting connected with me and once again I could hear these words: 'Ask me what your doubt are?' to which I answered, 'I have understood that you are directing this entire world. You are the power which makes mankind to take you as its God and worships you and you are always 'for' the welfare of everybody, every being, that is your big or prime concern. And what's more I have now known your real form also, you are the 'Star' with divine light which has the inherent capability to hear, understand and feel and to answer 'my emotions' again. But.... it's a big but in my mind namely, that if and when you had intended to answer my question, you ought to have first addressed that old woman introducing my name etc.to her and then answer my question or reply to my query. You are all knowing, omniscient then why did you not do as I suggested                                          above.
It fired a question at me in return, 'OK, tell me what your      name,      introduction      etc.      are?      '
I said 'Dr Sushila Choudhary' this is how you should have           called           me           then'.
It hurled another question on me with a sense of astonishment 'is this alone your real name?' And along with this, it reproduced before me the scene, that scene, where I had felt for the first time that I was 'out of my body ' and was feeling extremely light and was

full of joy, full with joy, with these words it also hinted cleverly that that happened to be introduction of my body, lying unconscious on the bed. Oh my! As if suddenly I came out of Darkness to light. It began become clear to me that that name was really the name of 'that' body, that unconscious body. My real self then is a different invisible power! "But then 'sir' you tell me -exactly what my name is? How would somebody call or address me, have my introduction who or what then am I?"

It reminded me of the scene of the star coming out of my body, as also that of the divine world in which so many people present in the form of stars were there and several of whom were known to me as my associates and my friends. Thus I could really feel that I was a shining star myself, full of energy or say a mass of conscious energy that in this divine state can see, understand and can create thoughts like the divine star mentioned above.

Still I told it -'Ok, I am a star full of emotions, thoughts- perception, but how to be convinced that the words you had uttered were directed at me, you had, in fact, never addressed me nor you had had my introduction!

In reply I felt the vibrations of the words of love-which were telling 'Having seen the place and the time, do you feel that there was yet another person there, who was remembering me (God almighty) and then being filled with anger and agitation, and was repeating in his or her mind the resolve to leave me itself forthwith                                    ?'

Now I felt that the capacity to think and understand that I was having was, far too, petty and superficial when compared with that of the divine star. In fact, that place had been peopled with those persons who had come there in order to lead a life of dedication and they were answering the questions in a positive way! but still that divine powers had made it clear that day 'the god is remembering that particular soul who has been feeling sore and had been striving to go away from there, There could not have been any one of that kind           present           there           so.' Then, does it mean -my real name is 'soul, Atma' and then I am identified by the thought content going in my mind at a given movement plus what kind of emotional responses are arising in my mind at that particular moment. Responses and resolves like these that come up in my, which much of my anxiety, got to be over and I then expressed my gratefulness to the divine star and I felt as if, it was telling me in response with giving a very good smile that "positive resolves are the basis of happiness and peace in life and is the way to keep connected with me in life".

In reply I told it 'Ok, I shall not even think of getting displeased with you now onwards. But then please guide me as to what I am supposed to do in order to be in your company' to this it replied 'I have already promised you to arrange for your studies' and before I asked him as to what particular studies, it pointed its finger to a big board which is kept hung in the front wall of the above institution which read "Prajapita Brahmakumari Ishwariya Vishwa Vidyalaya And The Spiritual Centre -from self-transformation to global transformation through Rajyog education"

Now it became crystal clear to me as to whole stream of studies I am to undertake for the rest of my life time, for that Supreme Power has selected, picked me up for such a noble and high task and has I recognised my worth and, that too on its own initiative had caused and made me pass through such rare experiences- experiences which have answered all the doubts and questions of my life appropriately and now they no more remain unsolved. Really how fortunate I am whom that Supreme Power has chosen to guide, uplift, protect and love.

    After the episode of the conversation between me and the superpower as detailed above my contact with it had come to be broken. But let me add that I had been treated to such a mystery of life which ended up with obtaining such a solution that my entire attitude towards life had radically changed, nay stood transformed. Now onwards, to me all my friends, members of my house and all the beings of the mankind appeared to me to be all 'conscious stars' only. And what I was now led to realise as how ignorant are all these people who forgetting their real self, are moving about imprisoned in the cages of their physical body and living a caged existence and dealing with life or transacting this business of life as per their varying cages defining themselves or labelling themselves as men and women, Hindus, Muslims and Christians etc. Whereas the truth is that all these separate entities, separate existence are all transient, fleeting, unstable, momentary and material. It is not their true introduction at all. We do not know our true self/form/nature -that's the reason, why most evils in life and the world flourish- evils like enmity, hatred, ego-clashes take place and cause sorrow. All those people who are prone to be afflicted with the above mentioned evils would not fall a prey to them and will not be miserable, if like me they know the real mystery'! The world would be a much better place to live in, if the people are awakened to the truth that I have experienced, the reality that I had been face to face with. All sorrow can vanish, all can become one that is united, and all can taste the real happiness and peace if they adopt the positive style of thought process and reflection. Now pondering over things of life often, I began to feel that the one point mission of my life has come to be perhaps this only -namely to tell of my experiences to others so that all can be conversant with the real form or truth of things and can apprehend that divine power as I was able to do on earlier occasions.

So now, once again I studied in detail about this institution and Rajyog, its establishment and its aim and objectives and with this I came to know that the supreme power is only one and one which is directing this world and it is that very power the same power which is running this institution also and the what is called the Rajyog here is the name of that methodology which enables every human being to help enhance his real spiritual awareness and knowledge and thereby to connect himself/herself with that Supreme divine power. With the acquisition of this Rajyog every man's soul get enriched with the noble values and noble, sublime qualities, there by attain/realise his entire and ultimate divine /serene/ perfect form where after attain happiness and peace.

By and by I had this realisation that the selection of the personnel for running this university and its various branches is also done by the same Supreme power. My selection to this institution by the divine star is the live example of this fact. Now, it thus becomes our sounder duty to make all other human beings in the world, irrespective of their sex, religion, colour or race to help them to realise and attain their real true self.

If we want to be successful in our effort to get ourselves repeatedly connected with the Supreme power and get the joy from the fruits of that power and get its esteemed guidance, in that respect for getting success then obedience to certain rules of conduct is important- example Satvik food (food prepared at its all steps with positive thoughts of peace, purity and joy), pure vegetarianism, cleanliness, celibacy -observance and regularly attendance of the classes of the positive thoughts of the institution and the mental and practical analysis of the knowledge acquired in the university and its implementation in the day to day life are some of the main points to be taken care of and to be strictly followed.

A few important events and astonishing experiences whereby that superpower drew me on to progress-

## When it protected us from a ruffian crowd

After having attended this conference my daily routine and the attitude towards leading life was completely changed I started getting up at 4 o'clock in the morning and in the Brahmuhurat, I would either have a dialogue with that divine star or would sit silently under its starry showers and watched it intently thereafter I would do my daily chores.

My mind now had begun to feel so peaceful and calm. It appeared to me as if I had been left with no questions or doubts to be answered or cleared anymore as if I had known now every mystery of this world and even if there arose any questions, they would be solved during my dhyan (meditation) time between 4 to 5 am in the morning.

Hardly a few days had passed when one day my husband who is a doctor was on his duty and he had a verbal shuffle with somebody. The thing took so serious a turn that within a matter of minute a big crowd gathered there. The crowd consisted of students and teachers staff who had come to the village in connection with annual sub- regional games and sports tournament. The entire crowd surrounded the hospital and swearing loudly saying that we will not 'spare' the doctor. I was on leave that day and was at home itself when suddenly the members of staff came and told me all about the incident, adding that the crowd could harm the doctor sahab and therefore I should do something about it immediately. In those days (1997) there were no mobile phones etc. Only local phones were the only source of talking over to others. I just focused my mind and attention towards the Divine supreme power and addressed to tell in my meditational dialogue that I wanted it to accompany me on the spot of the incident, as my guide.

I approached telephonically the Chief medical officer Sirohi and posted him with the facts of the incident and told him to report the matter to the police for our help, for in Kalendri the police staff is much too inadequate. I entrusted my children to the neighbouring care and departed for the hospital which was in the premises itself about 150 to 200 meters away. The staff that was outside too did not accompany me on account of the crowd and stone-pelting. I reached the main gate of the hospital all alone but undaunted. There I found that the staff closed the gate from inside, otherwise the crowd might have tried to enter the premises to beat the doctor. Without giving any reactions and perceiving the feel of the spot, I entered quietly in the premises by a side-gate opening in the delivery room and I found that everybody was so frightened. I consoled all of them that there is nothing to worry about and all would be well soon. There were a few patients also who were bogged up inside. I asked them to get out of the door-gate, but I found that a chunk of crowd rushing towards them I tried to explain to the crowd that they were patient and not the doctor and so they (the patients) might be allowed to go. They were all shouting that they would not leave the doctor and they were all carrying in their hands lathhis (sticks), hockey sticks, angle-iron pieces, stone pieces and what not! Looking at the entire atmosphere around when the crowd did not budge an inch from there, it fell to my lot to send the doctor away safely, hiding him and managing his ouster through a side gate opening on the fields and I did it so successfully and asked doctor-my husband to quietly start for the Sirohi district office by a vehicle.

Now to see/watch the hospital and to manage the crowd was a task that fell on my shoulders, it was time for the hospital to close too. The staff also wanted to go home, I told the staff that they would have to go out by the main gate itself and also to shut the gate of the hospital otherwise the crowd might rush in and cause damage to the government property but the staff was too scared. I came on to the iron-grill gate and tried to reason with the crowd, but some of them were adamantly saying that they would beat, kill the doctor. I once again remembered the Super divine power urging upon it to quieten the crowd, and explained at the same time some members of the staff to take a few people from the crowd with them and show them in to show closed rooms of the hospital and tell them that the doctor is not there he has gone and so now they too might go. I told the staff 'I am going home, but you should not come after me and go to your respective homes'. Outside the premises too I did not find any policeman or any person favourable to us. I opened the grill-gate and come out of it through one side. Some antisocial fellows to then enter the hospital premises along with the members of the staff, by the time they would have known that doctor sahab was not 'in' and that I was his wife I had already crossed the halfway home. The next moment I heard the sound of the stone pelted at me, but again without stopping and fearlessly I reached my house, close the door from inside, and now I heard the sound of the stones pelted at my door also. A few of the ruffians' bejade to put our scooter on fire. Looking out from inside I shouted at these fellows and swore threateningly at them for not so daring to do so otherwise they would have to bear the consequences. At this they made their way. All my staff and I were wondering as to how I had to walk up and walk on confidently, despite the enraged crowd and not a single stone hitting me.

In the evening other officer and police official had come down from the district headquarters. Quite a good number of members of the crowd was present there even then. And the crowd moved away from their only when an APO order was against us passed. In the meanwhile I had called my two children 4 years and 1 years too from outside, took them in from the rear gate and passed the time all alone. The next day we took over APO orders from the head office and started for Jaipur.

## He guided and supported me as my companion

Our new place of posting was the village Fefana,Tehsil Nohar district Hanumangarh- on yet another corner or end of Rajasthan from Sirohi as was near Gujarat border, what a sudden change in the life occurred?!
The life here began to be too monotonous. We had come here in the beginning of winters. Terribly desert-sandy area and the greenery at sporadic places would sharpen the teeth of winters. My daughter had become 4 years old but had not started speaking, the effect of her subnormal mental state was beginning to show up now. I felt so out-of-sorts there among poorly literate villagers busily engaged on their own work. There was nobody there to talk to--none who could come up to my IQ level. As for my husband, he would get bored when he came there. Watching films and indulging in drinking every day and getting up till late in the morning became his way of everyday life.
 Calling up the super power, (Khuda -Incidentally I had come to invent crux behind using this word as a mode of address to the super power now a days,

meaning thereby the person who himself (khud) comes to us on his own and gives his own introduction) I told it 'I want to go out of this place to a city, there was no chance of any progress or further studies here. How would this happen?

One full year passed in this situation of concern. I had now started studying for the preparatory exams for admission to post graduation course, for I had come to realise that there was no big recommendations with us for a transfer to the city, admission in post graduate course was the only option left in this context. I tried to persuade my doctor spouse to give some more time to the hospital and the children so that I could pursue my preparations more seriously and suggested that he should also read for the pre PG exam but him, my spouse refused point-blank to do so. He, on the contrary left giving time to the patients of the hospital and began to say that being husband, it was he who should first do the PG and also that he would get me admission next year, when he had become a postgraduate and that therefore, I could wait for another year -typical example of male-chaunism, chivalry ! But what can you do about it-you can only beat your head against the wall of your destiny. The class example of a typical creature called Indian husband.

From that day onwards, my husband even left looking after the hospital duty and instead shifted his books to a vacant staff quarter some hundred meters away. Now it became my added duty to send coffee, tea and food for him in that quarter. My problem got multiplied. He would come back from the quarter in the evening and would busy himself with watching films on VCR and would have a bout of drink in the night and would sleep. Whenever I wanted to talk about or discuss things related to exam studies he would invariably avoid it. Now I had to do everything all alone, looking after the two children, doing the duty of the hospital, making food etc. My worries and burden got increased. In the morning and in the evening in the village, often, the electricity would go off and then would come back late in the night.

I did not lose courage. I would get up at 4 o'clock in the morning I would do on meditation, take powers from the Khuda till 5 and 5:30 o'clock when the sun would rise, I would start study then for one and half hour. I would then get engaged in doing my daily chores. In the afternoon when the children slept, I too would lie down to about half an hour and then would got up and sit down to study for about half an hour. The Super divine power was helping me a lot- was the feeling I had. I had chosen only one book for my preparation and whenever I used to sit down to read then I felt that

It- Khuda was guiding me, as for example -'read this page, leave these questions' and I would do as per the Khuda's dictates.

Six months later I took the exams and I felt all along as if every question of paper, I had already read, my paper went off well.

A month later, the result came I got a phone call from my brother at Jodhpur. My husband picked up the phone, he told my brother, his roll number, the roll number was not there in the result sheet. He did not let me tell my roll number at which I shouted out my roll number on phone to which brother answered, this number is there in the first line itself which meant that I had got merit. Yes, true, mine was at number ten in the merit list of the whole state. Hearing this my husband got greatly disgusted and was filled with anger.

In my PG, I could have got any subject of my choice, my interest was in radio diagnosis but that would have meant our living separately. Looking to this, I opted for paediatrics from Jodhpur, for now I did not like gynec branch anymore.


## Guided me as a teacher and guide

My PG phase turned out to be full of tension and a very difficult time indeed. During my first year PG, I was able to see my children only in the night. Our HOD would get a paper presented by each one of the students at the state level. The preparation with regard to the presentation had to be done after the duty hours up to 11 o'clock at night in the hospital.

My husband was sore about the whole thing. He opposed it saying that there was no need to present any paper. As for me, I thought dropping the idea would mean displeasure of my HOD who might create problems in my way of the P.G. Moreover I too was interested in giving the presentation. Here again I sought the guidance of my "Khuda" the Supreme Power by calling him in my consciousness as usual. There upon the Supreme Power gave me the idea of the mode / methodology to be employed. That is why I would hear, with the help of the earphone, my recorded presentation again and again and would stand in front of the mirror and to critically observe myself I my performance I had to keep a check on the time & time Schedule also. All this was rather difficult.

In slides also, I made correction in them myself. My HOD Sir and I both were rather concerned to see that the Jodhpur team gave a good account of itself and may not put the name of the college to shame. But to me it appeared that "Khuda"-the Supreme Power was inspecting my work, directing me all the time, guiding me in this context and correcting me also wherever correction was needed. The first hand proof of this was that when

I went to Udaipur in connection with my presentation, and was about to give my presentation, my guide himself advised me "prior to your presentation do your meditation first and seek inspiration thereafter, for, after-all your preparation has been done on that line".
My presentation and the theme both were completely different from there of others. It was true, far from any external trappings, and the one which showed or highlighted the deficiencies in treatment. I had completed the presentation within the time prescribed. The loud clapping that followed was enough to prove that it was the best performance and I was the one who was going to get the gold medal. But no, having finished the paper-presentation, I just stopped for a moment and then continued my talk to say that we should not depend on allopathic alone, for in such cases even alternative therapies namely Dhyana, Yoga, Herbal medicines should also be tried. This extra sentence of 10 seconds against my expectation, was also included & considered for evaluation. However, I was able to bag the Silver medal being on second position in the entire State. I don't know how to thank and express my gratefulness enough to such a true invisible friend, my "Khuda "- who helps me out in every matter, at any time and gives

me courage & confidence and necessary guidance too.

## Gave an inkling of natural calamity

During the third year of the PG course itself when I used to go by scooter from my house to the hospital, the brake of scooter would invariably get automatically applied at particular place. The reason behind this was 'that invisible voice' which would say 'stop, look ahead, Ok, now go' when this thing went on every day, I came to suspect that soon there is something (foul) going to happen with here, I am scared and lo! Just a few days later in the year 2002 occurred that horriblast of the events of this century – the Tsunami. The time was the morning time around 9'o clock. The earthquake shocks of that day had developed a special sensibility/sensitivity in me, for now I can even realize the occurrence of even the lightest of such shocks, which often people cannot sense.

The places where brakes of my scooter got automatically applied, there was an old building which had got shaken badly during above shock and it could have fallen to collapse on the ground at any time, But no, I for one was feeling absolutely safe. And then further that building was later felled and a new building on the place had been constructed. That day was 26th Jan and the whole world remember it too well and not liable to be forgotten.

Now I had started calling addressing this "Khuda" of mine as 'Baba' (baabaa). It had known by now that this invisible super-power not only renders help, but like parents and good associates, gives affectionate warnings also to (be careful) and in every possible way takes great care of me.

## Protected me at a new/unknown/strange place

In the course of my P.G. years, my meditation had gone quite irregular which was telling upon my feeling of well-being. By now I had understood/realized the value of meditation. It was, for me, like a life force.

Once went to Goa on a visit of 'change' my spouse who was with one would not talk about the theme spirituality, nor would he allow me to talk about it. This had caused me an inside suffocation and upset. We were staying in a hotel just over-looking the sea-beach. It was 12'o clock in then night by the time we went to bed. But still I was not getting sleep. Before going to bed I had 'told' 'Baba' that I intended to do my meditation at 4'o clock in the morning on the sea beach. At 4'o clock early morning I woke up. It was still quite dark. I took up bath and got ready. I felt a slight suggestion of the dawn. Telling my husband that I was going out on the beach, I came down from the room out on the beach, it was all very quiet, out there, albeit a few sporadic shopkeepers could be seen their getting up for opening their shops.

However I began to feel a little fearful at the thought that if I sat at the beach care freely, somebody seeing me alone might play foul or cause some harm to me. Instantaneously, I addressed Baba & told him 'I want to me see/meet you at the beach and I have to talk with you a lot and also to engage myself in Rajyog. Please does something about it forth with'. Soon me hear some sound at my back? I turned back to find that there were two pet dogs of foreign  breed were standing behind & wagging the tails, as if they knew me too well. I was perplexed to find that there was no owner of theirs to be seen around the place.

I soon realized that this was Baba's contrivance/ tricks try. I sat down for meditation there without losing any time and began to meditate. The two dogs sat on either side of me as it I was their owner. I did meditation for about 45 minutes. And now since the day had dawned, the foot tale of the people increased. I got up now, and with me got up from their place the two pets also. I proceeded towards the hotel, when I turned back; I found that the two dogs had disappeared from there. I have not been able to forget this tell-tale incident over.

## Saved the life of a patient

I appointed in the ESI hospital at Jodhpur itself. The hospital did have a ward with beds, but there were no arrangement of experienced staff for looking after serious pediatric patients. In such a situation, whenever a serious child came to me, I would refer it to higher centers, one day a fellow – a father came to me with his 11-12 years old girl. His complaint was that she had been having fever for the last several days. I felt that all the necessary tests well have to be got done. So I referred the case for admission to other hospital. But the father was not prepared to take her to any other hospital. So he insisted that I should admit her & treat her in my hospital itself. At his insistence, I admitted her to our hospital, but with the condition that all her blood tests will have to be got done and the reports there of with have to be shown to me as soon as the reports came. I soon, in my mind, remembered & 'summoned' Baba, the divine power and urged upon him to take care of this child, as her father was not prepared to take her to another hospital & she had been ill for the last several weeks and looking serious. Starting the treatment with an antimalarial, anti-infective drugs, I visited her again at 5'o clock. The girl was better now. There was no fever either. I became confident that the treatment had begun and she was on way to recovery. In the night when I was cooking the evening-food, suddenly a thought that 'let me go& see that child again' flashed in my mind I paid no attention to it and went on with the task of cooking and arranging for dinner. When everybody had taken the dinner, the time was 9'o clock and again I felt that somebody as telling me that I should go and see the child again. At this I telephoned the hospital and asked the nurse about the child. Her answer was that she was absolutely fine and was sleeping after taking her food. The duty-doctor also enforced what the nurse had said adding that there was nothing to worry about. I got relieved & reassured.

Hardly 10-15 minutes might have passed when I once again felt that somebody from outside is goading me to go and check the girl patient again. Now this message was accompanied by such 'an energy' with which I was fully acquainted. I then said to myself 'what the matter is, the child is Ok, yes, then why I am receiving in my mind this flash (of energy)?'. Soon after in the next message I felt that the message was accompanied with the same vibes but the tone of the vibes was rather angry type & scolding, "Will you go to see the child or not? If you do not go, something wrong or unwanted is going to happen". I got rather frightened.

Now no courage was left in me to oppose this order, so I at once rushed on to the hospital ward, where the staff, patients all had gone asleep. I woke them up all and went to the bed of the girl to found that she was looking all fit. The staff too started telling me Dr. Sahab, you have got unnecessarily worried, there is nothing to worry about then I asked the girl's father that has her blood reports came? He said, 'Yes' I asked 'when? why did you not show it to me or the staff?' He had brought the reports & put it there at 8'o clock. I saw all the reports. I found she was malaria positive, plus her hemoglobin was also low, and on top of this, the dangerous thing was that the number of platelets were low to the point of concern (only 10,000 c/m). I was upset. It was already 11'o clock of the night. I could not have left the girl in this state and at this stage any more.
I rang up at emergency of the concerned hospital associated with the Medical College and informed that patients with very low platelets was being sent and as such necessary arrangements may be immediately made. Then I called the Ambulance

and explained to his father & others of the possible dangers, got then dispatched to the hospital. It is now that I felt a little relieved. Now it dawned on me why the flashes or directions again and again were coming to me since of 8'o clock they were being sent by Baba who was warning me of the delicate situation. Reflecting over the matter I thought to myself-There is a power, a super power that is more faithful, loyal, more disciplined and more alert and punctual than the human beings and is capable of helpings us out in and through any difficult situation, Yet, it is a pity that we do not associate ourselves with it and seek its help, its blessings & get blessed.

I could not resist my temptation to share the whole evening's happenings with me with my staff, the duty doctor, with the girl herself & parents of her. I told them in particular as to what I had experienced by way of flashes of messages in my mind. They all were pleasantly intrigued to hear all that I had told them.

## When I had been filled with fearlessness and courage forever

I was (in 2006) now looking whether I could be able to employ the instrument of Rajyoga (meditation), that is, that divine power of that

Supreme in the treatment of child patients suffering from the dread disease– Thalassemia, about which I had already started thinking seriously and in right earnest. In fact thalassemia the very disease of these very children was the theme of my M.D. Thesis, Driven by my faith in the Super Power I was gaining a strange confidence in myself and to believe the Super Power will be able to work, to liberate these thalassemia children, turn the dreadful ritual of infusing blood in their body again and again. For this I made a video also with the aim that the children may understand properly the mode of meditation and their ailment thalassemia. I wanted a proper, separate place for this project of meant where I can call these children and impart the practice/training of the Rajyog. For this I wanted a place in the hospital itself but I was not able to gather the necessary courage to go and tell (approach) the Superintendent about it.

About the same time, I had to go to Abu to celebrate the MILAN ceremony on the occasion of the Paramshakti Avataran Day. A renewed sense of discipline could be seen in my day to day life nee forth. I began to follow in right earnest my daily life- my morning meditation, all the principles for more organized studies and more pure and healthy food. My heartfelt desire was to have the firsthand experience of being face to face with and to meet that Super Power on the dais once again. I wanted to fill my mind and myself with that enriching, refreshing and enchanting experience and to comprehend the divineness of the energy, the power, the joy and love of that super star in me once more. Will this or could this be possible and will my Baba give his support to me in this endeavor? The Avataran program was going on, sitting there in the program I began to talks mentally to Baba 'Am I not eligible enough yet that once at least I can come to meet; see you from a close distance when you are seated on the dais and can feel you, feel your presence may be even for a few seconds. When nobody else on is there except for you and I'. At this juncture I got a message that Dr. Savita wanted me to go to see her. I got up instantaneously from my seat and reached her when she told me, "I have got a badge, the badge relates to the dais of Baba milan. I have received the hint just now from baba that I give you this badge. Pin it up, and go and meet Baba on the dais". My joy knew no bounds at this & lol! I was to go there forthwith. Now, a whole world of stormy questions began to rage up in my mind 'How good is baba! He really listens to the hearts of the people, what shall I say when I see Him. I am not even prepared for, that way... I do not even have a small flower to offer to a Power like you

etc.' and I could feel that the beats of my heart were getting faster; I had become so upset due to the suddenness of the whole thing. I had another fear up my sleeves namely that in my excitement to meet Baba, I may not be able to say what I want to.... lest this most important moment of my life may slip by with no result. A hundred thoughts like these ones were entrenching my mind and in this process of concern I was about to reach near Baba when I suddenly felt that somebody as if has switched off the button of my thoughts and a strange sense of total peace and calm and relief had enveloped my entire being and, further, that I was standing there right in front of Baba much in front of him and wonder of wonder no questions any more up in the mind, no wishes or desires, no ambitions or aspirations either a feeling of perfect contentment... And so soon my eyes had met the eyes of Baba. I had completely forgotten myself, obliviated myself, my entire entity, my total existence. I was not I and I did not desire/aspire for anything now. No want, no wish and why should; I need anything. I was getting everything over at and in that one moment. And then suddenly two phrases echoed in my mind yes, just sets of words. "Nirbhayee bhav, Nishchint bhav'
¼fuHkZ;h Hko] fuf'pr Hko½

(Rendered into English the words meant dauntless, fear nobody and be reassured, Have no worry) My sight was lost in the vision of Baba Then I moved forward. It seems the momentous moment of meeting my object of faith 'Baba' was over and as if the whole storm of aspirations had calmed down. Yes, a feeling of 'calm after the storm' I felt I was full of courage, I have no fear now, I am capable of doing anything with a feeling of Infinite joy, and boundless energy this moment gave a new turn, a new direction to my life.

I came back to my work place and engaged myself in the preparation of making a research plan for the cure of Thalassemia children by means of 'Rajyog meditation'. It was challenging but I felt I had the necessary 'daring' (courage) now and surprise of all surprises, I got the requisite support at every step. I was taking decisions at my own level itself-something which is not ordinarily done seen in the government service, People think twice before taking such initiatives. The ESI Health Director himself came over to 'release' my video and inaugurated the unit of research work and the chamber of Rajyog in the hospital itself. It was a big thing but to me so small now.

After six months hard work we found that the children reaped the benefit of the project in proportion to how much they learnt or understood of the Rajyog and how much they made practical use of it in their life and got wonderful results. Two girls of 12 and 14 years respectively practiced the hardest and at the end of the three months felt slowly and slowly a change and they did not have to get blood infused even once in the late three months. Which they otherwise used to do (one unit) every 12 to 15 days. In  one of the two cases even the shape of the liver and spleen began to become normal from enlarged size and the iron store (S. ferritin came down from 4000 u/ng to 2000 u/ng without taking any medicine for chelation. Speaking from mental point of view all the participants and their parents got very positive results.

However this Research work involved certain practical problems and difficulties like the frequent visits of the parents and the children from the far off villages and their stay and hence the financial implications etc. the research experiment had to be given up mid-way.

By practicing Rajyoga it became possible and easier for me now to establish mental contact or connections, particularly in those cases where the subject himself was a trainee of Rajyog. Even in regard to my own day-to-day things, if at the early morning time, in the Brahmuhurt (or Amrit Vela) I tried to establish contact with the help of Rajyog and to have conversation frequently it would always end up in positive results whether in terms of some wish, or some work or some dialogue. Not only this, I was by virtue of this connect, able to turn the atmosphere of home or hospital or the work places/office more conducive, friendly, favorable I can safely say that it, Rajyog mode is a very easy way/mode/method of making your life positive, friendly and favorable.

## When I rendered help to my father

My father had got angioplasty done on himself but he did not want to stay long on the hospital, so we came home it decided to pass a week with him itself. One night after three days, I felt while I was asleep that somebody had pushed me down from the bed and I narrowly escaped falling on flat on the ground, I somehow managed to stagger and stand up to find that there was nobody there in the room and my father was lying on his bed in a state of senselessness almost like a dead person. We used to keep one night lamp on, in order that my father may not have any difficulty in getting up or moving etc. So I could see clearly that he was completely like a dead person even the movement in the chest on breathing too could not be seen. My medical eyes were able to notice this much at least for sure. But what was curious that the whole room was full of a kind of furor, almost a storm raging in the room and I could clearly experiencing an energy force operating in the room and soon I could catch a set of wishful words  'save me somebody, help me out, Why don't you do something?' The whole things suddenly became clear to me that the words vibes were none else than my father's 'conscious self' which for some reason had come out of his bodily frame, but did not want to quit it (the native body). It is this very soul force that had shaken me up forcefully and caused me to wake up and made me feel the action of the body falling on the ground. In the course of those few moments, I was experiencing such powerful vibrations that they were not even allowing me to stand up properly and I felt as if the vibrations would enter my very bones and passing through them would shake me up violently as if bent upon making me fall on the ground. It was with great difficulty that I manage myself to stand up firmly. At this juncture I remembered Baba and expressed my wish of letting this Power to go back to its body. At this point I received cluster of thoughts from Baba addressing father 'Be quiet, Nothing has happened to your body. It was a temporary problem, it has been solved. The time of your death hasn't yet come and look the Supreme

Power itself is helping you go back to your own place'. And in a matter of a few seconds, everything was quiet again. My father's outside body's appeal and my prayer to Baba had brought fruits.

During all this while, I had been constantly watching my father's body but was not able to render any medical help because that 'Soul Force' had disturbed my poise, my balance and as such employing this soul therapy was the only choice/option left with me and I can say I was successful in it. I noticed that on one side the storm raging in the room calmed down, and on the other hand along with this I could guess some movement in the body of my father, who I felt was coughing now. I went to him and touched him, tried to wake him up. After a little effort he woke up. I asked him 'Are you feeling any problem?' I asked him so because I wanted to verify and express the truth behind this event, namely whether whatever had taken place was only my feeling or experience or that he has some feeling of it too. He was feeling so weak. In a very low voice he asked, 'Do you know?...' and here he stopped and began to think. I asked him 'whether he had seen some bad dream?' and further as to what happened to him. He again put it to me itself 'why did you wake me up? What had happened to me?' I avoided answering his query and said, 'Nothing, I was just going to the washroom and I thought just to ask you wanted water etc.' Then he became a little normal and opened to tell me, 'Do you know that I after having been dead, I have just become a live again. I was perplexed beyond words. I now heard from his mouth the fact of his being out of his body in a helpless situation and told him the entire story. Now we realized that on being out of our body if the consciousness does not leave the attachment of the body and treats it as a part of him, the great pain is caused. Whereas if or where the consciousness or the power of the conscious self 'knows it' that his body is only a means to it and that to enter it or to leave it is a natural process of which the soul is accustomed enough, the death became a normal process.

After a lapse of about nine years of the above stated event When he (my father) was at Sri Ganganagar and I was living at Jodhpur, My father had not been keeping fit for the last few days and his investigations were also due for that I was just going to take leave for that purpose. But about this time he had an attack of loose motions and he had become very weak, so we were just waiting for him to recoups
a little. On one of these days I was doing my duties in the morning at the hospital suddenly I got a

phone call from my younger brother telling me that father has become unconscious and that he was being taken to the hospital. But father was quite conscious in that morning as also in the last night I had talked to him by video-calling.

After putting back the telephone receiver, just a moment after it I felt that the things placed on my office table were shaking violently, the same storm raising from type of energy-vibration all around me as if a violent whirlwind, it was a kind of cyclone of energy wave moving around me and round the room. And with this a voice of wish was also heard to me 'I have not to give it up at yet, (it here stood for his mortal body). No, I don't want it, come, help me, you can? ' this was my father's voice. I was clearly able to recognize that his consciousness had quit body and further that this time his life-time had also become over. But he was not prepared to accept it. My younger brother, on the other hand thought that he had become unconscious but now he was dead, I was facing that whirl-wind that cyclone still, when I heard the ring of the phone again it was my brother's call. I had taken it now that he was going to inform me about my father's end.

The cyclone was still raging non-stop. It was not even allowing me to lift the phone even. Then I again contacted my Baba & I said, 'you are giving this soul the power of peace and come with me as I was about to tell my father that all is taking place well' but no-what I found was he had disappeared from the scene. Then I again rang up my younger brother.

My brother posted me with the detail that when he had taken Papa to the private hospital, the doctor refused to take the body out of the vehicle saying that he was (already) dead. He told my brother to take him home back. But my brother was a little sore, as he wanted the doctor to admit him at least and then try to make some lifesaving steps. So he arranged my dialogue with him on phone I talked to the doctor urging upon him to make an attempt at least for revival after taking him into the ICU and I told him that he had our Permission to do so. I urged upon him not to declare him dead forthwith. After great insistence from my side, the doctor admitted him, gave him electric shock and did cardiac massage on him also. And then when his heartbeat started, he was fallen on the ventilator. But my father continuous to be unconscious. But off course- now the whirl wind at my end had ended.

By the next morning I had reached Sri Ganganagar. The medical investigation clearly revealed that all his organs had stopped functioning. By means of medicines and ventilator his breathing and his heart beat was maintained up to minimum required level, his blood pressure was being still not under control. There was no hope of any improvement in the condition He had been in the same state since the day previous to it.

Now the problem was as to why he was being kept there now when no bodily organs were working or functioning. All members in the family were worried as to what was to be done the next. At last, because of my being doctor the whole decision was left on me as to what was to be done. And as for me, I knew in my mind that if my father had to quit his body without the consent of his consciousness we have to face further cyclonic episodes. Thereafter, I asked everybody to go out of the room and then I sat beside him and tried to put into his ear the correct position or the truth. I began to suggest to him that he is a conscious power, a whole unit by himself, whereas this body of his is only a means. I suggested him further that he was going to face to face with the Supreme Power and since now this body was redundant and had outlived its utility, he has to quit it or give it up. I tried to tell him that living in this body now onwards would cause pain to him, so he should not have any further attachment for it. Even otherwise all the medical instruments, tubes, needles etc. being used on him were causing pain and discomfort to him. And so if he so desired, we could liberate him all them devices and could take him home for which he will have to give his consent and say his 'yes'.

Now it was a little ironical as how a person, whose organs have ceased to work, if he is in a state of coma, could give his consent? But despite this I continued to put in his ears that he should make an attempt to give us his mind by giving us hint by moving his left great toe (making his toe to move up and down). If he causes his toe to move up and down, we will take it that he want to be taken home. But I told him that he was to move his toe by way of his consent only when my mother asks you for your consent and not when some other persons do so. Because this much effort was not possible by him in his this medical status. I further said, 'If you are not able to move the toe I will take it as that you are not listening to or understanding me In that case we will keep you here itself until you do not give up your own body & let it die. And since now you have to leave this body it would be better if you do it with you consent and in a more positive way.

I told or rather explained to my Mom everything and came with her to the hospital. First I let the Buas and other relatives to meet him and express their reaction. However my father remained all this through unconscious or without any senses. My Mom whispered in Papa's ear as we had planned. Papa, thereupon, in the presence of all caused movement in his toe. Mummy asked him the question as planned in second time and again he made his toe to move. The doctor attending him who was watching all this thought that there was some improvement taking place. He, the doctor reexamined him. But, sorry, he found that there was no movement of any kind in the body.

After all these stages had been crossed, the life support system was removed and we began to make preparation for bringing him home. After about 15 to 20 minutes of this, Papa's body was still, without any life sign but there was an atmosphere of peace all around.

The last rites were decided to be executed the next day, as my maharastra live resident younger sister was to reach in the night. She, my younger sister also practices Rajyog and she too had experienced the various stages relating to and involved in this Deha-tyaga episode of Papa. In our society, daughters do not go to the graveyard but we the two sisters decided that we would go to the funeral place (graveyard) and shall stay there till the whole ritual or the last rite went over. This was because we both felt that for our father's conscious-power to see own body vanishing into the panchtatva (the five fundamental /basic elements) would be certainly painful affair and as such he will have to have the courage enough and the necessary cooperation for facing the situation. All the formal programs were taking place so peacefully too far we had reached the burial place. My sister and I both took our seat on the carpet spread in the verandah. Copying us our Bua and a few other women of the family also managed to reach the funeral place but they did not have the courage enough to stay over to see the dead body flamed. When the time to put the dead body to flames came then I felt that a small child had emerged out of the pyre and came over to where we were seated and stood trembling out of fear. I remembered Baba through my usual meditation mode and then began to look at the child figure. It was infect my father's soul which in his consciousness or mind was appearing to be the form of an innocent but frightened child. For by now I had understood that the mindset in which the soul (consciousness Power) happens to be at the time of appearing itself at the particular moment, will determine its form image. I looked at my sister, she too seemed to share what I had felt she nodded in agreement. Then both of us began to meditate. We remembered Baba. Baba too appeared and stood near the soul of my Papa. Baba had come in the form of an old man shadow surrounded by a white shine of light. Seeing the Baba there, my father soul suddenly began to hide itself behind him (Baba) who caught Papa's finger tight in his hand. Just as a child wants to see a horror serial on the screen and yet tries to hide behind his mother the scene was something like that.

And when my younger brother proceeded to perform Kappal -Kriya, the shadow of the consciousness of Papa, sort of, completely broke up and to curled itself up completely behind that 'old man' shadow. During this process, we both the sisters, we kept helping him by expressing our blessings. At the same time we went on addressing Baba also. After the Kapaal-Kriya, as if the shadow of Papa adopted a completely 'dethatched' attitude and hinting the shadow of Baba to move away from there and then in a fraction of a second both disappeared, god -knows where!

<u>When the definite time of visit etc. in a matter which was bogged up in the process, was prophesied</u>

In the year 2004-2005 I was posted at the E.S.I. Hospital where mostly lower middle class level

patients used to come for treatment. I found in them utter lack of education and so a high incidence of diseases. The family planning strategies too had failed to give them due desired relief in terms of limiting their families.
Looking to this situation, I started educating them in respect of the bad effects of excessive sex and teaching them the value of a celibate life. However before doing this, I had tried to gather the opinion of the people of various age groups, segments of either sexes on the subject of indulgence in sex. I got a good feedback also and inspired by this and taking advantage of this I prepared a research paper also on this theme (celibacy), duly supported by the references from ancient literature on the subject prepared a 'folder' also in which I had tried to highlight the need for observing celibacy after the completion of the family. If was emphasized in the folder that due control and due sex discipline would result in physical, mental and social advantages. It was attempted to apprise the couples of the various modes involved in it.

I wanted to exhibit this folder in my hospital and the Gynec hospital for the benefit of the public. But surprisingly all the hospital & the doctors and even my Superintendent were all reluctant in permitting me to do so and for which they did not forget to give references of the various departmental rules prohibiting such a display. Whereas the important fact at my level was the folder was being liked and received well by the common men and women who were rather curious to know all these things in detail.

It was an ironical situation after a long drawn attempts of several months I was disgusted to realize that this world would not let me ..... Or for that matter .... Anybody to do something off the track, something new, respective of the fact whether it was a useful thing/idea/suggestion /proposition.

On one of my meditation calls to Baba in the morning I told him that with great effort and labor and hard work I decided to undertake the task of educating the people and of relieving themselves of their sorrows and ailments, but I am so disgusted to find that the people of the world are washing off all my labor which is very unfair, won't you Sir not help me in this pious task that I have undertaken?'

A few days later, in the course of my morning yoga session, Baba gave me the order that I should prepare letter in respect of my research work about family welfare and a copy of the folder and take these papers to the collector's office and present them there today itself, explain the things over to the officer concerned. I was surprised to realize this now that I had learnt to feel the difference between the vibrations caused at my end when sending and expressing 'my resolute energy, and the vibrations caused when receiving the bliss full grant of the resolution.

I prepared the letter, went to the office of the Dist. Collector, and met the officer concerned (ADM-II) who used to deal with the matters relating to health. The meeting went off smoothly the officer was rather surprised to know that the higher officers of the Health Department had been so hesitant, reluctant to facilitate the exhibition of material so useful for the common man for the messes. Having known the vital details, the officer was receptive enough to not only give me written permission for exhibiting the information on the board but also made separate official budget available for making the board besides complimenting me for my valuable research. He did not stopped that, but he went a step further. After the board was ready for being installed, the officer even took initiative to inaugurate the board himself. Wasn't all that just wonderful!

It may be noted that later I participated in the national level and other conferences to read this very research paper of mine, thus drawing the attention of the Health department in particular and of the society in general.

# When 'he' directed me to write a book

I have been receiving communication from the Baba to the last one year that I have to write a book and that the book is supposed to be written in English language. The very thought that I was required to write a book in English everglade, a little too heavily on me and I got a little nervous to think as to low I shall be able to write a book in English. At that points of time it was not clear to what the theme of the book would be and what its form and purpose would be.

One day suddenly while on my way from home to hospital I noticed a board on which was written 'Spoken English Class'. I had not seen then board earlier, Was it a god sent thing? Yes, certainly it was. I was eager to learn spoken English those days so I could fulfill the above thought of Baba and the class was on my way. Some NRI Indian had started the classes. I made enquiries and joined the class. It was the first batch and I was one of 4 or 5 students thereof. The class was run for one month after which it was closed down. But it proved a boon for me. I could learn a lot in this short time. My hesitation in speaking English was now gone. That NRI also got a glimpse and experience related to Baba. This sudden arrangement was, as if, contrived for me by that Supreme power to whom I was highly obliged and whose blessing and grace I was a recipient of. How great of that Supreme Power!

Soon after this I had to go once to the Head office of brahmakumari institution. In the course of a meeting there, I came to know that a book was proposed to be got written on the theme 'value empowerment' in respect of adolescents and the youth, I got a hint from a resolution from the above that I had to take up this proposed task. Even otherwise, all these days I was quite a lot upset about the social situation of the adolescent and had wanted to prepare some teaching material in that behalf. And lo! My wish had been fulfilled I first wrote the book in English Language, for which I learnt how to operate computer and mobile and I was able to type the whole book on the computer. Then, from it, I prepared its Hindi edition/ Version also.

Now on the basis of this book we have planned and prepared a seven day workshop. Under this project, we are supposed to spend about one hour per week in a school or institution with the students and by mean of discussion the theme is properly explained to them. The concept of values and the spiritual consciousness is introduced to them. And the feedback that we are getting is excellent and encouraging. Doing and experiencing all this I get a real relief and peace of mind. The reason as I have found is that today each and everybody is caught up in a morass of problems and complications. How to obtain real happiness in this illusory world-man is ignorant of the right path and stands therefore strayed away. In a situation like this when is introduced to his own self, that is, when he is made aware and conscious of his own potentialities, his own possibilities, his own strength on the one side, and when on the other side the supremacy, the supreme might of that Supreme Authority the ultimate Power of is revealed to him, then an unanticipated contentment can be seen to glow on his face and then from his mouth the words of real gratefulness come to be expressed and that is the basis of his contentment, his relief. And this spiritual knowledge is the I feel, is the need of every human being in this world. Yet it is an irony that man gets strayed and lost for want of necessary awareness and knowledge regard his own self and in regard to that Super Power called the Supreme soul (God).

Again it was 'he' the Baba, the Supreme Power who inspired me to write a book depicting on my spiritual experiences and is supposed to convey my positive message to the world. But let me share this fact with my readers that by the blessings grace of that super power I was able to write the book in terms of the hints I had been receiving from the cosmic Super Power up and above us, Baba had continued to be kind to me up to writing of this book itself.

## Some important points-

You and I, we are all power centers of Consciousness who through the instrumentality of own physical bodies express our thought, emotions in this world in the form of what is called our personality. We all like to acquire the uplifting feeling or sentiment of peace, love, piousness, and power and then to distribute all his two other. This is our basic/fundamental/ native nature and this, then is the basic truth of all human souls, irrespective of whether they belong to this religion, caste, community, province sex or to that.
And because we are the form of resolute energy, that is, made of, or comprising of that itself we are obliviously immortal, indestructible, invincible and so we will continue at the same time to participate in the worldly activities also because this is a part of our nature and we cannot live without transacting this business of exchanging thought and sentiments in our day to day life. Resolution is

energy and energy scientifically speaking never gets destroyed nor created, only it changes its form. The soul or the power of consciousness is in itself a whole, an entire unit. But without the aid of the body it cannot produce words or actions and can only feel one-sided activities or processes like hearing, seeing and emotional perception of things, it cannot however reply, react or answer back, But of course it can influence the emotions of other person if in the memory somebody gets connected with that consciousness, then that conscious power can transmit its thoughts, feelings to the mind of that person remembering him or of the person getting connected mentally.

When we (souls) are out of or alienated from or external to this physical body, then we souls see the world objectively/ dispassionately/impersonally and can understand the sentiments, feeling of the other human beings properly, unmindful of the words, noise of words that accompanies their conduct. The human souls after all, have experienced things while still living in the physical body and further because the soul can also watch and comprehend emotion/ thought/sentiments it is able to appreciate the sum and substance of circumstances. In fact the act of seeing & feeling things is not done by the eyes ..... , it is done by our soul operating through sense perception and since this sense perception which is developed in every soul by virtue of infinite life time experiences leads us to the understanding of the state of peace, noise, taste and other similar conditions ........... what starts amazing us is the point that the same soul/spirit while living in the body was not able to know what was there in the other people's mind, but now body less soul can read the thought / reaction/ sentiments/ feeling of human beings. This is the secrete of how Rajyog makes you able to understand other persons mind-set and enhance your intuition power and thus increased rate of success in life.

As for the souls separated from the body in accidental deaths we have a tendency to interpret and dub them as ghosts/evil spirits etc. But what is surprising is that on separation from the body the soul becomes disabled to speak or to give reactions, but then the big question is why we become afraid to face these souls? My answer to this 'Why' is : the resolute Energy, Power of the alienated soul, as acquires an amazing ability to read the mind-sets of human beings i.e. souls in their body as described above. Although these Souls are able to read or control the minds of only those human souls who are all the time remembering the alienated souls or are lost all the time in the thought of these alienated souls. And again only in respect of those resolves or wishes which come to stay in their minds (of free soul) at the time of such separation i.e. death. And here we can understand that in case of a death by accident or suicide etc. how negative the thoughts of the victim should be seeming to be at and that juncture of death-time, in regard to the accidents, its causes and its implications. When such negative thoughts arise in the mind of the living man are caused to ember they will of course frighten the man and This is what, in our weak moments, we call as the effect of the ghost /evil sprint of that entity or soul. similarly if somebody in the memory gets connected with the consciousness of a person or of a free soul irrespective, however of the fact whether that person is just in front of him or is at a distance of thousand miles away from him the main thing being that the line of mind from both the ends is should be clear than the particular conscious/soul energy can transmit its sentiment/ thoughts to that other human being. This is what is in the language of science is called Telepathy.

On the other hand it has also been noticed that in case of a particular person, good positive spirits or soul force are competent to and are inclined to give correct guidance to the subject. Such spirits are given the name/status of and are remembered as kuldevtas (family gods/legends).

The soul powers always like to live well in the bodies because in their body-less states they are just invalids only. Living in the body or leaving it are things which are controlled by an invisible system what is called KarmaVidhan and the agency directing this is none other than the Super-Power. That is why the above mentioned influences whether positive or negative of free souls are effective only up to a certain period of time or interval where after they automatically become weak or even vanish from the scene when as these sprits or souls enter another body.
The good thing about this is that whereas the soul gets concentrated on its thoughts/mind-set/sentiments it becomes stronger. Then why not while living in this very bodily frame itself, should we learn that method by which we can make our soul concentrate on its real form and thereby make our resolutions powerful and turn them into action so that success becomes a part of our life.

And one more thing that when we are all fated to live on this planet, then why not we live with love, good feelings and cooperation mutually because a happy and cheerful life is what everybody wishes for. Let all of us feel realize that the whole world is a family because all the souls are to reside here itself. And so let us resolve to make this earth and this nature green and free of pollutions as also to put climate and solar energy to positive and constructive use.

Now, every human soul after being dead, i.e. after being out of the body invariably does meet that Divine Light star that mass of holy light. That bright lighted 'Living Star' tries to make us understand that we are all made of and bound by the bonds or resolutions of love. Here the word 'Love' stands for and involves selfless service and of care for others, care with dignity and perfect freedom of dissemination of all our thoughts. Here the word 'Love' does not stand for physical or physicality of love. Here then we all are the forms of that one single phenomenon called Divine love. The Supreme Power is an ocean of love. 'He' fulfills all our needs of love or the lack of it. His love gives us true contentment. So much contentment that we do not wish then to have any love or beg of any love from other human being. He is the Supreme Giver. After meeting Diving star we feel like giving to others what we have got from him.

My thesis based on my experiences Readers, is that in order to meet that mass of Divine light we need not court or woo death or need not die. We can, while living this life can experience him, can experience his company, can apprehend his proximity, can experience his divine touch of love, can realize his presence, can perceive that mass of Divine light-the shining star, can 'meet' him. It most certainly gives or lends a positive attitude to human life or human beings and in accordance with is entailed man's behavior with man. Which can obliterate all sorrows of this earth and can initiate waves of happiness and make life paradise-like place and this planet a treasure of pleasure, divine pleasure.

One step in that direction is expected from everybody, for all this reality, truth and no imagination. Because at this time 'He' the Divine star is more eager to connect with each of us.

## Making Death and the post-death journey happy or joyful

What is death? When the conscious 'resolve' energy gets set outside this body, the process by the world is called 'death'. The closer the connection of a person with this 'real energy form', the more its effect on this process of death. If while we are living we should try to practice this auto suggestion that. 'I am a conscious energy mass who is doing all the worldly things/acts through this body, then we will have as much attachments with our own body as we have it with other tangible things of ours, say like car or mobile or ornaments. When we lose any of these tangible things we do not give up or sacrifice all our happiness - we only very lightly say that 'does not matter, will buy another'. In the same strain when our body has some ailment, or is hurt in the accident, we can also talk in a similar way. Never mind, I will go in for another body'. This will be a consolation which will not be painful. The noteworthy thing is that if you have practiced whole life that You are body and not knowing about for soulness or conscious energy form then when you face process of death or if you die or give up your body thinking that it is 'you', then the death or the parting will be painful affair. The subtle point here is that In fact what he really is, he himself does not fully know. He does not fully know his strength, his qualities, in such a situation he will not be able to accept the new situation objectively or dispassionately he will find that what he (his body) is not, is going to perish and he will be sorry about it. In disgust he would say, 'how stupid of me to have always thought that's body is everything'.

Secondly, when due to excessive attachment, the resolve that he will make at the time of death, that very chief sentiments/ mindset will became a fixed phenomenon in terms of the energy mass/soul to enter the new body and due to repetition of the same sentiment, the journey of the next life rule also became a cause of concern until unless the person concerned is able to know the reason. I have experienced this thing in many of the cases which came to me. I cannot describe all of them here for want of the consideration of privacy as also for want of space and for fear of the book becoming more voluminous.

In the above context, I would of course, like to add that each one of us ought to keep in mind the fact that death never comes with information. It comes suddenly and uninformed. But Death is certain to come. So it is important that we should take ourselves as conscious Power and in the wake of this feeling we should stay happy, joyful and calm and with peace. For, it is just like putting a DVD or video CD on 'pause' suddenly and restarting. For restarting would mean that you could re-start the CD it will be resumed from the very point when it was left earlier. This analogy applies aptly to our death and rebirth issue also, that is, if you leave your body with/along with a feeling of peace, contentment and joy, the next part of your life's journey will begin too with a note of peace, happiness. Who is there among it us who does not nurse a desire like this? Everybody does.

Whatever is happening now in this world is a repetition of things that took place before a certain period and that too without any change and exactly the same reproduction, unless the human soul willfully makes any new change. This wheel of change is an eternal feature and is also indestructible and is formulated under certain principles and the said principles too are true for all times and apply to the souls also.

This principle is related to the aspect of translating our pious wishes/resolution into action. The kind of thought, deed and word we would employ in case of others will rebound and come of us back with the same intensity, the same delicacy of sentiment and in the same strain of voice by way of reaction. Now it is we who will have to decide as to what kind of behavior to except from others, from nature. If we expect a certain kind of behavior from them, then we too on our part, will have to do the similar unto them. What we give will come back to us in return. After understanding this mystery we will be able to understand as to why somewhere there is heaven/happiness on this earth and why at other place hell/sorrow. And the way or method of removal of the sorrow or hell-like things i.e. the method of change too would be in our hands.

There is an Authority in the world that is higher than all the rest and which perpetrates justice. But of the time frame or time period and may take several of our births in dispensing justice, we think that justice will not be done to us at all or justice has not been done to us as yet or that this supreme authority is not capable of doing justice. The conclusion is that this Supreme Authority ultimately does not fail to give us justice. Since this Authority is beyond time and since it has to deal with immortal souls who are themselves or their journey of births and rebirths and thus the accounting of their deeds may take several life times. We doubt that justice will at all be done. But no justice is ultimately done. It may be delayed but it is not denied.

What is most amazing but true fact is that all these things were revealed or told by that Divine Light Force not to me alone, It can reveal this thing, or is very ready to reveal this thing to anybody too who, with a little effort, wants to get connected to it. And so if with such a little effort we can get in touch with that Divine Force, it will be worthwhile doing that effort and get connected with it at this time when we are living or alive. That Divine Star itself is always much too willing to get connected with us (during our life time of course) in present era.

## Self-Change

What was the effect of this entire spiritual journey on my life is something that I would like to tell my readers here in the paragraphs below:

Before I had undergone the 'experience of getting connected with myself away from my body,' I happened to be a very shy, tight lipped, introvert, timid kind of women who gave prime-must concern to (keeping of) peace. Several questions, doubts, complications were of course, there in life, but I would bear them all without sharing them or telling about them to others. I would keep them to myself and was by nature Cheerful? No, I was never. For all my temperament and Sanskaras, I would blame only myself, It a kind of guilt feeling and I would question myself why after all am I like this'?

But, believe me Sir, as I went past these unearthly/spiritual experiences, an amazing degree of change I clearly began to be felt by me in my own self. I was able to perceive the definite differences in my personality. I was turning on into being a bolder, certain, assertive, frank, confident and reassured person. I had now got free of questions and complication, doubts and despair, and that the reason why I began to feel happy and contented and cheerful keeping my internal peace in fact was my primary concern or priority even now, but that is not out of some out word force or compulsion. On the other hand I had realized now that my peace, my contentment and my cheerfulness themselves are my real power It is only through this that I can give something to my life as well as to the lives of others I can bring about a change in my life as well as in that of others. I can now very naturally communicate or have conversation with that Divine Star/ Energy mass of light and I can clearly feel its direction/ guidance sought in respect of myself as well as that in respect of others.

I have now no fear in my mind of the word 'death'. And I am always on a look out to do now whatever I have to do in this journey of life of mine. Yes, to do it soon now, for the simple reason that I may not have to be regretful or discontentment, a sense of in completeness or unhappiness at the time of my death, and so I am gladly ever ready to give up this physical body of mine.

This has given me a new vision, a new direction to take my life on to, with the result I find and live every minute of my life rewarding and every wish of mine accomplished. I do not now while away my vows, energies and time in insubstantial things like negative conversations, verbal tussles, trivialities of relationships and worldly matters, going in to details, stress producing situations, petty ego clashes, or deep-seated jealousies/ rivalries/ enmities, prejudices – all these things, as if, have vanishes from my temperament vanished miles away.

There has come in my relations a streak of detachment, as it were. That does not mean that I do not love people; rather on the other hand I have come to love people more dearly, for now I have come to understand that all those relations/relationships are ever going to be with/ around me and therefore I bear my responsibilities and duties towards them with all my sense of commitment and affection, and if I do not get its due reward /result, I do not cry or grieve but now I have come to know/ believe that what I am giving to others is I had got from them and am returning it now. And if even if, in return, I am not all to get the due love and honor from them I am not worried, for it will definitely get the same in future when the right time comes. I have reason to believe that the 'sentimental energy' which I shall send will certainly come back to me in the same measure through some medium at some future time. So now it will lie in my choice to spread in this very birth or in some future birth the kind of mind-set/ thoughts that I wish to get back from others and from nature in future.

While passing through these experiences I came to, learn to feel, by and by, my star-light form, or shall I say, my Sukshma form or my angelic form and further that I came to learn to know how it had initially assumed the form of a 8-9 years old innocent child, and later that of a young man and now that of a matured person. Feeling the existence of my own Sukshma or angelic form I feel great relief, peace and lightness. This is my assessment/ evaluation form also. Whenever I find myself too much involved in the worldly or negative things or atmosphere, then I clearly find that my angel form starts getting melted or becoming faint. Then I once again practice acquiring (acquiring) positive atmosphere of peace, love, sympathy, then the form itself becomes more glorious. As it comes to become more glorious my influences on the atmospheres around and in fact and in every act, activity of life gets on to become more positive and one, liable to give successful results.

Thus, for my part I have found a clue to the way of healthful living I would rather say that my body starts keeping the same way as my Soul does. If (soul) I become negative, my body would be afflicted by various ailments.

Now I have come to the conclusion that every soul is its own doctor of the body as well as its own. If one is keen one, can seek guidance from that Supreme Light, House of Divine Energy and can liberate itself from its bond of physical ailments and other problems and the same theory I am using for treatment of chronic illnesses of my patients and getting amazing results out worth of the type of diseases.